POSTER IDEAS and BULLETIN BOARD TECHNIQUES: For Libraries and Schools

FOR YOUR INFORMATION . . .

Many illustrations in this book may be used interchangeably by both librarians and teachers . . .

Display arrangements in numerous instances are easily adaptable to other subjects and materials . . .

Descriptive notes, names of artists, designers and photographers associated with borrowed illustrations, have been used where forwarded . . .

Method processes listed are not always in step-by-step sequence. Readers should follow their own judgment and convenience . . .

Attempts were made to obtain diversified examples of bulletin board art from schools in various parts of the country, for the purpose of supplementing the good work being done in Maryland, but such photographs were not available . . .

BEGINNING BOOKS

LITTLE BEAR'S FRIEND

A FLY WENT BY

POSTER IDEAS
and
BULLETIN BOARD TECHNIQUES:
For Libraries and Schools

by Kate Coplan
Chief, Exhibits and Publicity, Enoch Pratt Free Library

Original Art by Constance Rosenthal
Lettering Art by Charles Cipolloni

OCEANA PUBLICATIONS, INC., DOBBS FERRY, NEW YORK

PRINTED IN THE UNITED STATES OF AMERICA

CONTENTS

Books by Kate Coplan

EFFECTIVE LIBRARY EXHIBITS: How to Prepare and Promote Good Displays
POSTER IDEAS AND BULLETIN BOARD TECHNIQUES: For Libraries and Schools

Principal Photographers: Sydney Sussman, Fred Worthington, William Ochs
Book Designer: Leo Martin

To my family with love

— K. C.

ACKNOWLEDGMENTS

In a work such as this there is naturally a large debt owing to many people. To Constance Rosenthal, particularly, and to Charles Cipolloni, I am deeply indebted for their remarkable talents, "know-how," zeal, unflagging devotion and enthusiasm. And in the same breath with Mrs. Rosenthal must be mentioned her patient, long-suffering husband, Philip, who put up with countless inconveniences and ran interference for innumerable projects associated with this publication.

Warm thanks are due various officials and personnel of my beloved Enoch Pratt Free Library: Mr. Edwin Castagna, Director, for constructive reading of the manuscript; the Board of Trustees, for permitting occasional related correspondence on Library time; Mr. James K. Dickson, Head of the Fine Arts Department, Miss Marion Bell, Head of the General Reference Department, and Mrs. Julia Certain, Head of the Education Department, and their capable staffs, for assembling pertinent literature.

Out of their broad experience a number of persons in the fields of education and librarianship have made important contributions, through lending illustrative material, indicating areas of coverage, giving valuable advice and suggestions, answering letters, or offering sympathetic moral support.

Listed alphabetically, in true library fashion, they are: Mr. Maurice H. Annenberg, President, Maran Typographers; Messrs. William L. and H. Elliott Becker, of the Becker Sign Supply Company; Mrs. Dorothy S. Bowling, Public Relations Representative, the New York Public Library; Mr. William Braam, Assistant Director

of Public Relations, the Brooklyn Public Library; Dr.
George B. Brain, Superintendent of Public Instruction,
the Baltimore Public Schools; Miss Clara E. Breeding, City
Librarian, the San Diego Public Library; Dr. Angela M.
Broening, Director, Bureau of Publications, the Baltimore
Public Schools; Mr. James E. Bryan, Director, the Newark
Public Library; Mrs. Aileen Cipolloni, Baltimore artist; Mr.
George H. Cordry, Jr., Wicomico (Md.) Senior High
School; Miss Anne M. Davison, Teacher, the Baltimore
Public Schools; Mrs. Helga Eason, Director of Community
Relations, the Miami Public Library; Jack Engeman, Bal-
timore Artist-Photographer and Author; Miss Eloise M.
Frain, Display Artist, the Glendale Public Library; Mr.
Robert D. Franklin, Director, the Toledo Public Library;
Miss Gertrude Gscheidle, Librarian, the Chicago Public
Library; Mr. G. Alfred Helwig, Director of Curriculum,
the Baltimore County Board of Education; Mrs. Frances
Henselman, Assistant Libarian, Administrative Division,
the Long Beach Public Library; Miss Helen Hermon, Area
Director, the Baltimore Public Schools; Mr. Joseph Hill-
yard, Supervisor of High Schools, the Baltimore County
Board of Education; Mr. George Horn, Art Supervisor,
Secondary Education, the Baltimore Public Schools; Mrs.
Downing Kay, Pre-School Head, Grace and St. Peter's
Parochial School, Baltimore; Miss Dorothy G. Keesecker,
CORE Coordinator, Middle River (Md.) Junior High
School; Miss Esther King, County Librarian, the Public
Library of Annapolis and Anne Arundel County; Miss
Johann Klick, Librarian, the Baltimore Public Schools;
Mr. James League, Teacher, the Baltimore Public Schools;
Mrs. Ruth Levin, Baltimore artist; Mrs. Esther Mann, Prin-
cipal, Mt. Washington Public School, Baltimore; Mrs.
Hortense D. Meister, Public Relations, the Public Library

of Cincinnati and Hamilton County; Mr. Richard Micherdzinski, Director of Art Education, the Baltimore Public Schools; Miss Anna C. Miller, Vice-Principal, Eastern High School, Baltimore; Miss Kathleen Molz, Public Relations Officer, the Free Library of Philadelphia; Miss Jean Moser, Supervisor of Junior High Schools, the Baltimore County Board of Education; Miss Alice Norton, formerly, Public Relations Officer, the Public Library, City and County of Denver; Miss Beryle Kay Orman, art education elementary school student, Maryland Institute of Art; Mrs. Evelyn Orman, formerly of Mt. Saint Agnes College; Mr. Harold Osborne, General CORE Chairman, Golden Ring (Md.) Junior High School; Mr. Timothy Owings, Instructor and Head of the Art Program, Junior and Senior High School, Gailsville (Md.); Miss Mary Perentesis, dynamic Instructor and Chairman of the Art Department at Eastpoint (Md.) Junior High School; Miss Esther J. Piercy, Chief, Processing Division, Enoch Pratt Free Library; Mrs. Elizabeth Rawlings, Art Teacher, Eastern High School, Baltimore; Mrs. Mary Ellen Saterlie, General CORE Chairman, Stemmers Run (Md.) Junior High School; Bernard J. Schmidt, Police Commissioner of Baltimore; Mr. Myer Site, Art Teacher, the Baltimore Public Schools; Mr. Bert N. Snow, Public Relations Officer, the Los Angeles Public Library; Miss Nettie B. Taylor, Director, Division of Library Extension, Maryland State Department of Education; Miss Sarah L. Wallace, Public Relations Officer, the Minneapolis Public Library; Miss Dorothy Waugh, Director of Public Relations, the Montclair Public Library; Miss M. Bernice Wiese, Director, Library Department, the Baltimore Public Schools; Mrs. Beryle Wiseman, Teacher, the Baltimore Public Schools; Mrs. Howard Wood, the Talbot County (Md.) Free Library.

Grateful thanks must go to Mrs. Emily Hagan, talented Pratt Library exhibits artist, for her constant and ever-efficient cooperation in connection with the "How-To" Helps, execution of several displays, and modelling of various techniques, on her own time.

Others in Pratt's Exhibits Division who cooperated from time to time were: Frank Cipolloni, Lorraine Stonesifer and Vincent Hammel.

Special thanks are due three members of my family: Miss Edith H. Coplan, for her excellent typing help; Miss Fannie A. Coplan, for the loan of her law office and equipment, and Mrs. Bessie I. Steinberg, for her expert messenger-delivery service in connection with preparation of the manuscript.

To all these and many more too numerous to mention, I herewith express my everlasting appreciation.

Kate Coplan

FOREWORD

by
EMERSON GREENAWAY
Director
The Free Library of Philadelphia

For years the by-word in the library world has been—if you want to know about library exhibits, first ask Kate Coplan of the Pratt Library. Almost thirty years have gone by since the now famous windows at the Pratt were first used for exhibits, which of course entailed the use of posters. Now the library world is to have printed access to Miss Coplan's thoughts and ideas on posters and bulletin board techniques.

In a world that is display conscious, unless library exhibits and posters are done with a professional skill, it would be better to forget them. In most exhibits, posters play an important part. Even posters alone can be used most effectively to interest the reader in good books and reading. It takes skill to create a stunning poster; it likewise takes skill to effectively use a poster with books to the greatest advantage.

It is no secret that considerable library time can be and is spent on bulletin boards and posters. Administratively the question can be raised: How much time should be spent on these activities, and also, can the effectiveness of this work be measured in terms of exciting individuals to read more? The end result must be the determinant, for what Miss Coplan is writing about is not interior decoration. If librarians use posters and bulletin boards as interior decoration, they had better stop, for more effective permanent decoration can be obtained by other means.

The problems of poster and bulletin board work will vary according to the size of the library. The small independent library will be at the greatest disadvantage, for there will be fewer staff members to call upon for this activity. Here, perhaps, is an opportunity to secure the services of a friend of the library, experienced in display work, to provide this service as a contribution to the community as well as to the library. Whether it is a friend offering his services, or a member of the staff doing the work, it is best to plan bulletin board displays and posters that can be used over a fairly long period of time, thus getting the best mileage out of the work involved.

The larger libraries or active library groups or associations may have annual in-service workshop programs for effective poster and bulletin board work. There are few central exhibits departments that can cope with all the requests for either material or assistance that come in from the public service staff. Therefore time spent on display work and techniques must be telling. I emphasize annual workshops, not only because of changing staffs, but also as a means to introduce new ideas, techniques and materials. Nothing is more deadly than to have the same kind of techniques used over and over again. If this happens you will lose your audience and one of the most important purposes of display work is to hold your old audience as well as to get a new one.

We must remember that posters are primarily to announce events or to give specific information. They depend on color, line and typography to attract and hold the attention of the viewer. Bulletin boards, on the other hand, should be developed around a central theme on which the library is prepared to furnish the reader with materials from its resources about the topic in question.

The person preparing the bulletin board will draw on all kinds of materials—prints and pictures, as well as three dimensional objects such as books, models and handicrafts. He will use high color tones and contrasts to catch attention.

Some bulletin boards may convey their purpose, but it is usually best to have a brief statement embodying the purpose of the bulletin board. Copy should be brief, interestingly written and easily understood. Be sure to have type that is large enough for all to read, and place it in a position where it can be easily read at eye level.

Remember that this, along with all other exhibits, must be for an educational purpose. It must not be slick or cute. Its effectiveness will determine its usefulness.

The alert librarian doing this work will watch the good educational institutions, especially museums, and at the same time remain aware as to what can be adapted to our purposes from the world of business.

Poster and bulletin work, well done, is an art— and it is also a challenge, and when successful a joy to both the creator and the viewer.

Emerson Greenaway

PREFACE

by
ROBERT IGLEHART
Professor of Art and
Chairman, Department of Art
The University of Michigan

The publishers' lists of new books for teachers grow longer and longer. Those of us who teach have no remaining hope of keeping abreast of the literature of educational research, advice and revelation. I know one elderly professor who has given up the unequal struggle, and now carefully files his copies of professional periodicals to read after he retires.

But despite this flood of books and articles, some critical areas of the teachers' work have been curiously neglected or inadequately treated. To one of these areas Kate Coplan addresses herself in this book. I am pleased to write this brief preface because I am convinced both of the great importance of visual materials in education, and also of the pre-eminent qualifications which Miss Coplan brings to her subject.

By the time I had reached junior high school in suburban Baltimore I had read everything which I considered of consequence in our neighborhood branch library, and began to journey to the main building of the Enoch Pratt Free Library in the city—a Victorian monument full of the gloom appropriate to books and learning.

But when the Pratt moved into its present building in 1933, conservative Baltimore was astonished to note not only that the library was full of light and air, but that across the main facade was an entire block of show windows, much like those of a large department store.

Nearly every new library now includes display facilities, but so far as I know the Pratt—a remarkable institution in many ways—was a pioneer in this field. In the Pratt windows Kate Coplan experimented with, and found ways of attracting public attention to library resources, new books, special fields of reading, events of literary importance, and topical publications.

The windows rapidly became and remained a pleasurable part of the city scene, and their appeal and effectiveness has been many times made clear by circulation figures. During the period when I was studying in the city I had the good luck to be associated, in a small way, with the displays, and could observe at first hand the intelligence and skill which went into their planning. Under-staffed, under-budgeted, and limited in space and materials, Kate Coplan met successfully the same sorts of display problems which are likely to confront the teacher.

We have all been made aware of the great value of visual materials and resources in the classroom; film strips and slides have become familiar in nearly all schools, and the possibilities of television are the subject of intensive study. Many of our textbooks begin to be made as attractive as we hope to make the knowledge they contain. And the teacher has often become extremely skilful in the use of these professionally prepared resources.

But even when, in the most favored situations, the teacher has ready access to the finest of such resources, there remains an area of visual education which is the teacher's own. Professionally prepared materials can help present information and stimulation, but the work of a particular group of children—their responses and expressions—often needs to be organized as a display for the benefit of the class or the school. And there are the many interests and concerns of this particular class for which no professional materials exist, and where the teacher is the best available expert. We have all come to expect that the competent teacher will be able to prepare a display, hang an exhibition, decorate a room for holiday use, make up a chart or a poster, and help the students in such activities.

Teachers should be able to do these things; they are within the reach of anyone and they are all immediately important to the educational experience which the school should provide. But neither in our teacher-education programs, nor in-service work, do we typically offer much help or practice in developing such skills.

As a result, many teachers feel insecure in relation to this area of the teaching job, and neglect it altogether. In many schools an already overburdened art teacher is asked to tackle projects which should, by their very nature, be the task of the teachers and classes out of whose activity they have grown. A display which is the culmination of a science unit is properly part of that unit. To permit its dislocation is to lose part of its educational value. I am confident that this book will be of great service precisely because it is addressed to those with modest skills, less experience, and limited time and resources.

It is educationally important that we use display and visual techniques, and it is educationally important that we use them adequately. Visual learning and visual expression are central aspects of a school program—especially so in the elementary schools. We are still, as Whitehead wrote almost a quarter of a century ago, "too exclusively bookish in our routine." We still do not sufficiently take into account the importance of things as against abstractions, and the visual as against the verbal. This does not at all mean that the abstraction and the word are lessened in importance, but that we should recognize the way in which both are strengthened through direct and exciting experience.

The good classroom should have its own quality and its own life; it is the children's immediate world. This is why it should be made not only comfortable and healthful, but vivid and stimulating. That part of a child's life which is lived in school should be no less real, and should develop values no less real, than his life after the school day is over. The contribution of good visual materials and displays to this end are enormous.

But it is just as important educationally that whatever we do be done well and attractively. This does not at all mean that we must rival the professional, but it does mean that we do our best and help our students to do their best. For the visual aid and display must always have two effects: on the one hand they convey information and on the other they touch the esthetic sense.

The power of a work of art depends on the absolute unity of these elements. The teacher must be more modest in his intent, but we must not regard the information only as important. If we neglect visual quality we may cancel out the initial impact of the information; or we may convey the information and at the same time vulgarize the eye. It is for this reason that those of us whose field is art are concerned with and involved in the visual element throughout the school program. But although the art teacher should be concerned, it cannot and should not be his task to do all that needs doing.

Finally, we often forget that the major educational value of visual materials accrues not to the spectator, but to the creator. The exercise of organizing ideas, defining points and ordering the presentation of information is in itself rewarding and illuminating. The teacher who is prepared to approach this part of the job competently and confidently, and who can help his students to do the same, will be rewarded in the coinage of learning. The delight of principals and parents is pleasant, but the real objective and real attainment is the increase of excitement and attainment in the school world of the child.

CHAPTER ONE / COMMUNICATE THROUGH VISUAL DISPLAY

The persuasive influence of effective visual presentation grows stronger each year. Recognizing this fact, industrial and other profit-making organizations are allocating increasingly larger portions of their advertising budgets to this important tool for expanding markets.

Taking a leaf from the commercial notebook, libraries and schools, along with other non-profit agencies, are developing greater awareness of the vital role which dramatic display can play in widening readers' horizons, and enriching learning experiences.

By the use of simple designs and inexpensive materials, along with the mastery of a few easy how-to-do-it techniques, even the least experienced librarian and teacher can carry out display ideas clearly, effectively and successfully. Added skill will come with practice. The school of trial-and-error speeds the learning process if we are alert to profit from our mistakes.

Today's much-maligned villain of visual display, in so far as libraries and schools are concerned, is the poster—focal point of many a bulletin board designed to stimulate interest in library resources and classroom instruction.

All too often librarians and teachers with little art training and less talent are called upon to produce posters that tax their abilities to the utmost and consume precious hours which they can ill afford to give, both for the planning and execution.

Bulletin boards to the uninitiated are even more frightening bugaboos, with their vast expanse of undecorated space full of pitfalls for novices charged with transforming them into helpful channels of communication.

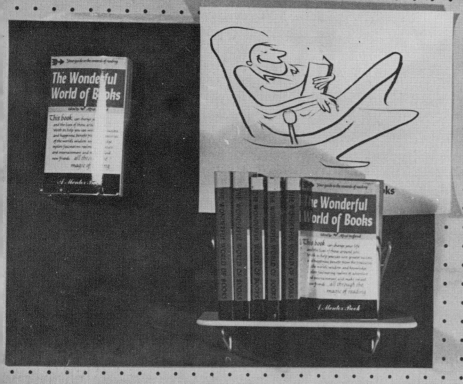

EXPLORE THE WONDERFUL WORLD OF BOOK

The Wonderful World of Books

PLEASURES OF READING

READING AMONG FRIENDS

READING MORE EFFECTIVELY

TOWARD WIDER HORIZONS

THESE BOOKS MAY BE BORROWED

PEG BOARD EXHIBIT
The New York Public Library

Only a handful of the larger metropolitan libraries are geared to cope with this type of effort, through their public relations staffs and exhibits equipment. For the most part the preparation of posters and bulletin boards means one more heavy burden thrust upon librarians already busier than the proverbial one-armed paper-hanger, who are struggling with innumerable duties involving work with the public and behind the scenes. Especially in the smaller libraries, where the chores grow infinitely faster than Jack's storybook beanstalk, does the job of poster or bulletin board prove a formidable undertaking.

KEEP ON LEARNING

Concerned with inescapable routines, the selection and ordering of book and non-book materials, classi-
fication schemes, cataloguing services, loan work, reader's
advisory and reference work, indexes, bibliographies,
budgets, shelving, weeding, records, statistics and a host
of other matters, librarians in the smaller communities
understandably have scant time to devote to stimulating
displays.

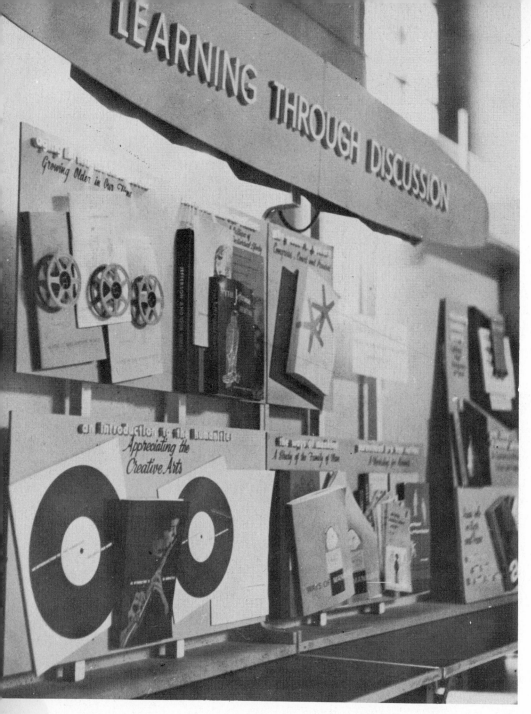

As for teachers, who also carry an overwhelming load, the onerous addition of displays sometimes falls in the category with the straw that broke the camel's back.

According to a study made by Dr. Arvid J. Burke, of the New York State Teachers Association, the typical teacher's work week generally approaches 50 hours or more. Not only do teachers conduct classes and supervise

THE STORIED PAST

OOKS ABOUT ARCHAEOLOGY AND HISTORY

pupils, but they also help students with their problems, correct papers, prepare lesson plans, confer with parents, attend P-TA and professional meetings, cooperate on school-faculty projects, and perform many other assignments.

Dr. Burke points out that nearly 23 per cent of the elementary teachers do not even have a free lunch period, since they are called upon to supervise children at lunch or at play. Moreover, the amount of clerical work required by activities both in and out of school is gaining constantly.

It is hardly surprising, therefore, that under such circumstances, many teachers and librarians find the necessity of initiating and executing displays a difficult, often frustrating, experience.

Further, unless they are particularly gifted, despite their best efforts the results are likely to prove dis-

BOOKS ABOUT ARCHAEOLOGY AND HISTORY

Materials and Colors
Paint, roller, transparent ink, cutout letters
Black, red orange, olive green, tan, on white

Method
1. Roll on olive green paint
2. When dry, roll on transparent ink in red orange, for a stone-like quality
3. Large letters shadowed and touched here and there with white lines, to give chiseled, "old" effect
4. Letters comprising bottom line have had white paint applied to edges with point handle end of paint brush, to give "eaten-away" aged look
5. With easel attached to back, the piece may be used on a shelf displaying books on the featured subject

Fred Worthington Photo

INDIAN TALES AND TRAILS

Materials and Colors
Cardboard, tag board, construction paper
Black, gray, white, yellow, red

Method
1. Simulate book with cardboard and decorate with construction paper
2. Make head and feet from tag board, features and decorations, in simple shapes, from construction paper
3. Thin strips of construction paper form shoe ties.
4. Put cardboard easel on back of book, if display is to be free-standing

Fred Worthington Photo

appointing and ineffective, from both the artistic and practical points of view. Obviously, there is little profit or satisfaction in carrying through a time-consuming project, only to have it turn out amateurish in appearance and incapable of accomplishing its mission.

One of the primary purposes of this book, therefore, is to turn the villain into a hero—to demonstrate that good posters may be done with a minimum of time, energy and money, tailored to fit the subject to be projected. Another major aim is to change the bulletin board chore into a challenge—to assist hard-pressed librarians and teachers in achieving more meaningful communication of their ideas through visual interpretation.

Briefly, these pages set forth ways and means of producing simple, striking posters and bulletin boards which can win and hold attention, yet are easy and inexpensive to do. There are practical suggestions on captions, design, materials and techniques, short cuts, tricks of the trade, with emphasis on three-dimensional arrangements. We cannot stress too strongly that even librarians and teachers with little skill and experience in display planning and preparation, should be able to obtain attractive, exciting results by following the procedures indicated.

ADVENTURE BOOKS

Materials and Colors
   Black board, chalk, white letters, plastic (acetate), ink, poster paint
Method
   1. Draw illustration with white chalk, using a guide for half circle and a cone shape for the hat
   2. Draw eyes, nose, mouth, hair, hand, with chalk, then with a wide brush superimpose white poster paint
   3. Apply bright-colored inks over the poster paint, giving a free, water-color look
   4. Cut plastic to cover head, simulating a space helmet, and pin down

Fred Worthington Photo

Ideas and illustrations may be used as presented, adapted with any modifications desired, or as a springboard to the reader's own imagination, talent and ingenuity.

JAPANESE FESTIVAL EXHIBIT
The Denver Public Library
Display by Janice White
Photo by Bob Gordon

But if the librarian's or teacher's artistic abilities are limited, it would seem sensible to lean on and learn from the examples cited, if they tie in with the subject at hand. Let us remember that there is "nothing new under the sun." Virtually every new idea is based on something that has gone before. The rendition, the interpretation, the adaptation, may be fresh; but somewhere, somehow, at some time in the past the basic idea, it is safe to assume, has already been introduced. With practice and experience, know-how will be greatly expanded.

WHAT'S IN THE NEWS?

Materials and Colors
Felt, newspapers, construction paper, pins, stapling gun or tacker
Olive green, turquoise, magenta

Method
1. Felt stapled onto bulletin board, then strips of the fabric *pinned over staples for neater finish (pinheads touched up with matching paints)
2. Large caption letters cut out, rubber-cemented to white construction paper, and placed in position

Note: Current events articles and activities can be featured

*Where stapling is not practical, felt may be glued on

Sussman-Ochs Photo

In order to make this volume as useful as possible capable, discerning practitioners in both the library and educational fields were consulted, to help determine where the greatest needs lay. Their valuable and constructive suggestions have received serious consideration, and in many cases were adopted. As a result the following chapters reflect the broad scope of public library service, as well as the diversified school curricula.

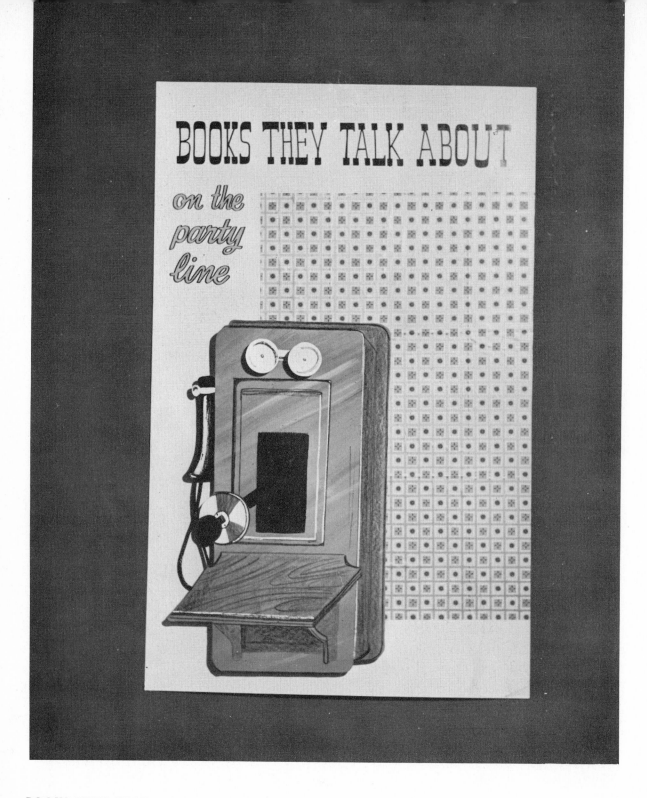

BOOKS THEY TALK ABOUT ON THE PARTY LINE

Materials
    Patterned paper, cardboard,
    rope, paints, ink

Method
1. Piece of patterned paper from dime store mounted on white cardboard, in good design
2. Telephone cut from cardboard, painted to look authentic, and pinned away from back, to give 3-D effect
3. Rope used for telephone cord
4. Hand-lettered caption in related style period

Fred Worthington Photo

CHILD WELFARE

Materials and Colors
> Book jackets, cardboard, string, velvet bow, paint
> Tan, black, blue (in addition to jacket design colors), on white

Method
1. Jackets with stiffening cardboard inside, pinned away from board
2. String lines to hands, which are also pinned away from board for 3-D effect
3. Velvet bow in child's hair

Fred Worthington Photo

NATURE NOTES

Materials and Colors
    Wallpaper, construction paper, hat pin,
    thumb tacks, paint
    Black, orange, yellow green, red, on
    white

Method
    1. Bits of patterned wallpaper make butterfly,
       top of acorn, worm, and spine of book
    2. Hat pin holds butterfly to book
       Black thumb tacks serve as eyes for the worm

Fred Worthington Photo

DIET AND NUTRITION

Materials and Colors
    Construction paper, ink, paint, cardboard
    Black, yellow, orange, tan, blue, on white

Method
    1. Flat paper shapes, hat folded for shadow
    2. Center of book pinned away from board

Fred Worthington Photo

GOOD MORNING, GOOD NUTRITION

Materials and Colors
Cutout multi-color letters; plastic bowl and spoon proportionate to the display; kitchen towel; black cloth tape; construction paper; pictures of children and breakfast foods; cardboard
Red, light and dark blue, yellow, on white

Method
1. Small cutout multi-color letters applied with glue to plastic salad bowl and spoon from dime store
2. Kitchen towel "table cloth"
3. Children's faces cut from discarded magazines; picture of girl second from left slit under arm, and book inserted to give dimension (book made of cardboard and paper)
4. Black cloth tape holds colored construction paper and picture-photos together in shape of an arrow

Fred Worthington Photo

DO YOU KNOW THESE NOTED COMPOSERS?

Materials and Colors
 Cardboard, paper strips, cardboard circles of various colors, pictures of composers cut into circles, names of composers lettered on small paper strips
 Black, white, orange, turquoise, purple, yellow (circles), on white

Method
1. Staff lines made of strips of paper or cardboard
2. Cut circles of cardboard a little larger than pictures of composers
3. Paste photos of composers onto cardboard circles with rubber cement, double-coated
4. Paste on names of composers

Sussman-Ochs Photo

CIRCUS DAYS AND WAYS

Materials and Colors
    Cardboard, construction paper, felt-tip pen, colored inks, wool yarn
    Black, orange, yellow, purple, hot pink, on white
Method
    1. Legal seals as decoration for trousers, facial features, and elsewhere
    2. Wool yarn for hair
    3. Lines made with felt-tip pen
    4. Line around figure coordinates with letters
    5. Colored inks inside letters

Fred Worthington Photo

HOW TO USE THE CATALOG

Materials and Colors
Cardboard, ink, legal seals, catalog cards
Orange, tan, yellow, black, white, red
Method
1. Large red legal seal for "asterisk" to left of caption directs eyes to explanatory units below, and small "asterisk" on bottom sign reading, "Ask at Reference Desk If You Need Help"
2. "Arrows" are thin strips of cardboard with small triangles glued on

Sussman-Ochs Photo

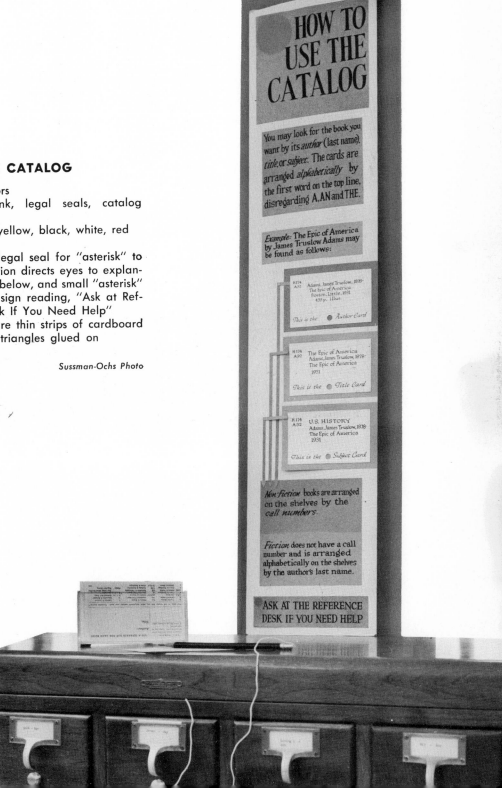

RECESSED EXHIBIT
Long Beach Public Library

BACK TO SCHOOL

Materials and Colors
    Tissue paper, cardboard, paint, ink
    Red, black, white, dark pinks
Method
    1. Lines of book pages printed with edge of cardboard
    2. Bells of tissue paper, outlined to look as if they were ringing

Sussman-Ochs Photo

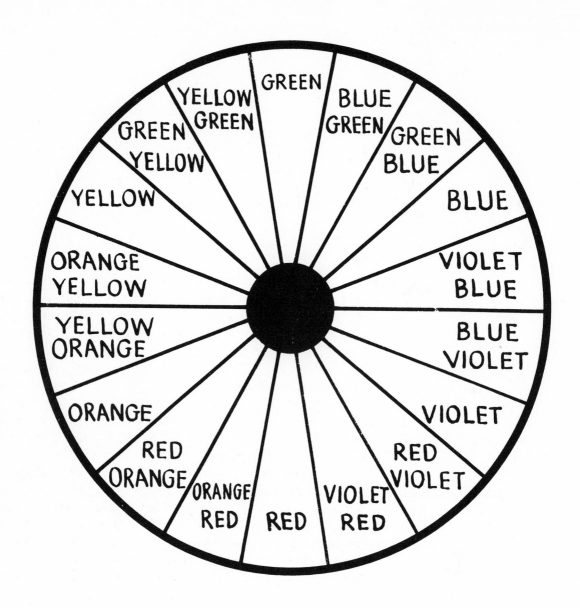

COLOR WHEEL

Indicating the wide range of tones and intensities available to display workers

CHAPTER TWO / COLOR NOTES

Since ancient times color has been a dominant force in life. In one form or another it has served and influenced man through the ages, making his home, his surroundings, his place of work and worship, his whole world more beautiful and meaningful.

Imagine, if you can, existence without color. Spring, for example, without Nature's multi-hued floral displays; earth without green grass and trees; sky devoid of heavenly blue; sunsets minus the decorative pinks and purples. The end result would be drabness, monotony beyond measure.

It was Sir Isaac Newton, discoverer of the theory of gravitation, who first offered an explanation of color phenomena. Using a glass prism in a darkened room, he experimented with a ray of sunlight as it entered through a slit in the window shade and passed through the transparent triangle. When the sunlight penetrated the prism, dispersion took place, producing the band of beautiful colors known as the solar spectrum.

These colors are red, orange, yellow, green, blue, indigo and violet. The strongest values in the spectrum—red, blue and yellow—are called the primary colors. Secondary colors are those noted between the primary colors—violet, green and orange. Adjacent to the primary and secondary colors are the intermediate colors—violet-red, violet-blue, blue-green, yellow-green, orange-yellow and orange-red. All colors, therefore, are variations of those in the spectrum, from which colorists took their cue in devising color wheels, charts and coloring materials.

Complementary colors are any two opposite, or contrasting colors, that furnish completeness to each other. For example, when two primary colors are combined, the result is a secondary color. Then the remaining primary color becomes the complement, or greatest contrast, to the secondary color.

If red and blue are mixed to produce purple, yellow—the primary omitted—becomes the complementary color of purple. Further, red is the complementary color when blue and yellow are converted to green, and blue is the complementary color when the primaries, red and yellow, are mixed to produce orange.

Color means many things to many people. The bright, vibrant colors have a tendency to stimulate, while the soft, subdued colors promote restfulness and repose. Contrast adds interest. Pleasing effects can frequently be achieved by using the strong, intense colors to accent neutral or quiet tones.

As pointed out in this writer's earlier book, "EFFECTIVE LIBRARY EXHIBITS: How to Prepare and Promote Good Displays," the value of color psychology is significant. During the summer it is wise to feature the "cool" colors—the blues, greens, violets, grays and white. The winter months call for proper selection and arrangement of the "warm" colors—colors in which the reds, oranges and yellows predominate.

Harmonious use of color in design is desirable, for colors which do not balance well may irritate some viewers and fail to make the desired point or convey the projected message.

However, at the present time when contemporary designs thrive on unusual color schemes, there is a definite trend toward combining some of the colors formerly regarded as clash colors—for example, blues and greens, magenta and orange, or pinks and reds. Some of these, such as magenta and orange, conveying excitement when used together, can be toned down with white to produce the arresting colors that are so attractive in modern design.

Although the standard shades and primary colors are always good and should be used often, especially for children's posters, variations in color combinations are fun to experiment with. While red, yellow and blue are juvenile favorites, other colors may also be used successfully.

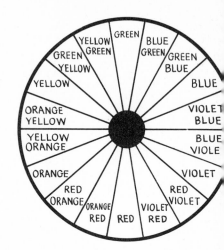

For instance, a Christmas poster done in red and green may be made more interesting by using, instead of the traditional hues, a red with purple added, along with either an emerald or olive green, or perhaps even turquoise. This type of treatment assures attention, for the color presentation is "different." Also, when introducing a new project, a "shocking" or unusual color scheme is likely to elicit maximum interest.

In general, to lighten a color, add white. To darken add a little of the complementary color, or black. The former is preferable, as black has a tendency to dull the color, whereas the complementary will make it look richer. In order to mix a "warm" gray, add a trace of orange to black and white. If faced with the problem of making two sharply contrasting colors, such as red and green, harmonize, add a bit of red to the green and a little green to the red.

To obtain vivid shades of color, the German-made "Pelikan" brand hues may be considered. These are most intense and come in a large selection of poster paints and inks.

Tissue papers, which can be acquired in rolls of 36 sheets, each measuring 20 by 30 inches, also are available in a wide range of delightful shades suggesting interesting and eye-catching color combinations for those who choose to work in this attractive medium. In fact, just seeing the colors as represented by the tissue rolls, bottles of ink or poster paints on the market, is likely to dispel any timidity felt by display beginners, and whet the appetites of incipient designers.

In producing posters, water color and casein paints are often used, with water as the thinner. Occasionally, for a more durable mural or out-of-door effort likely to be subjected to the elements, oil paints are employed. The latter may be "Bulletin Paints," available in most display or hardware stores, and costing about twice the price of regular house paint. This medium, made with a rubber base, covers smoothly, stays where it is applied, and does not run or spread.

Color charts are usually available free on request in paint, hardware and art supply stores. Attendants, if approached during non-busy hours, are glad to advise on special problems.

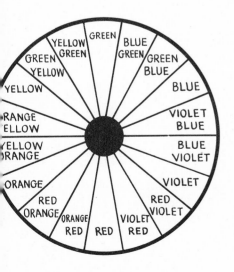

Both water paints and oil paints should be stirred well before using. And if they stand inactive for any length of time, they should be stirred frequently, to maintain full color strength.

Paints mixed with water, exhausting moisture quickly, are likely to look a shade lighter when dry. On the other hand oil paints, which require a minimum of four or five hours drying time (overnight is better), appear darker when dry.

For poster and show-card colors, employ sable hair or camel hair brushes in assorted sizes. If variation of treatment is indicated, the sable hair is preferable, since it comes to a finer point and makes a finer line than its camel hair counterpart. Sable hair brushes or quills (brush ends with plastic sockets, for which handles may be made or bought) are best for oil paints. The sizes are similar to the camel hair brushes.

When working with oils, have a palette handy to test paint consistency, to wipe off excess and assure evenness of distribution when color is applied to the respective art areas.

In mixing paints you may want to match later, write down the exact proportions of colors used, for future reference. Should you want to duplicate a particular one, of which you have a small quantity on hand but lack a record of its component parts, the way to do it is this: Place two equal squares of white paper or cardboard side by side on a black mat. Then put a sample of the old paint on one square, and a sample of the newly-mixed paint on the other, altering the latter until the exact shade desired is attained.

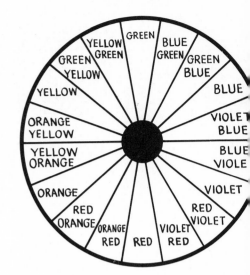

SOME ATTRACTIVE AND UNUSUAL COLOR COMBINATIONS

Blue, Green, Purple and Magenta
Emerald Green and Magenta
Olive Green and Magenta
Olive Green, Turquoise and Magenta
(The above make especially good Christmas colors)
Olive Green and Blue (Any shade of Blue lighter than Royal)

Lavender, Pink and Pale Blue
Turquoise and Olive Green
Turquoise and Emerald Green
Turquoise and Blue
(All the above colors go well with Purple)
Purple and Orange
Hot Vivid Pink and Bright Orange
(A Vivid Pink toned down with White, and Orange toned down with White, gives a Strawberry Pink and Orange Sherbet look, a luscious effect for posters and bulletin boards featuring cool summer drinks)
Pink and Yellow (spring "flowery" colors)
Orange, Magenta, Pink and Olive Green
Orange, Magenta and Olive
Orange, Black and White } These are masculine
Tan, Black and White   in feeling
Black and White (Always a good, bold combination)

Of course, Black and White may be used to advantage with any vivid shade. And White is especially desirable as an accent on displays. It lends a note of freshness, an important factor in getting attention. For this reason, particularly, White is an excellent background choice.

OTHER COLORS THAT GO WELL TOGETHER
Rose, Gray, Black
Blue, Gray, Pink
Yellow, Green, Blue
Purple, Green, Blue
Rose, Navy Blue, White
Blue, Lavender, Black
Yellow, Purple, Lavender
Red, Yellow, Black, White
Dark Green, Turquoise, Yellow, Black
Tangerine, Turquoise, White
Pink, Dark Green, Yellow
Pink, Brown, Green
Aqua, Brown, Pink
Pink, Imperial Blue, Rose
Brown, Orange, White, Turquoise

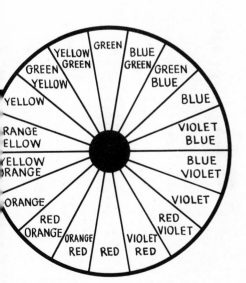

Lavender, Yellow, Black
Maroon, Jade Green, Pink
Brown, Green, White, Tangerine
Maroon, Yellow, Light Blue
Navy Blue, Deep Pink, White, Turquoise

Let the mood of the caption or theme of the display suggest the color scheme, and determine whether primary, conventional or unconventional colors are to be used.

Persons lacking experience with color paints, may find the following information useful. It is taken from "EFFECTIVE LIBRARY EXHIBTS."

IF YOU WANT TO MIX YOUR OWN PAINTS . . .

Red + Yellow	= Orange
Yellow + Blue	= Green
Blue + Red	= Purple
Blue + White	= Powder Blue
Red + White	= Pink
Black + White	= Gray
Purple + White	= Lavender
Orange + Purple	= Brown
Brown + White	= Tan
Orange + Red	= Tangerine
Yellow + Orange	= Golden Yellow
Red + Purple	= Turkey Red
Black + Blue	= Navy Blue
Green + Yellow	= Jade Green
Green + Small Amount of Black	= Forest Green

To make a color lighter add White
To make a color duller and darker add Black, or:
A trace of Green will dull Red, a trace of Red will dull Green
A trace of Yellow will dull Purple, a trace of Purple will dull Yellow
A trace of Orange will dull Blue, a trace of Blue will dull Orange

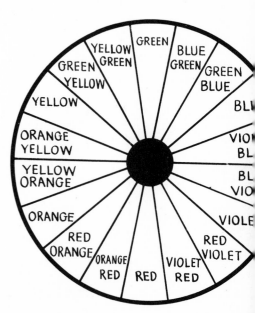

NOTE: In combining paints, use small amounts at a time, and stir well after each addition.

When matching waterpaint colors, it is advisable to let a small sample of the mixed paint dry thoroughly for best comparison. Tones have a tendency to lighten in the drying process.

CHAPTER THREE / CREATIVE POSTERS

The three principal ingredients of creativity—inspiration, imagination and ingenuity—are basic to posters, as they are to any other type of good display. But a generous helping of the two latter elements can often compensate for a scarcity of the first.

Possible poster ideas abound almost everywhere, in daily contacts, conversation, events. An elderly woman patron of a public library, for example, might return a copy of "Jane Eyre" with the comment, "That's an old favorite of mine." The alert librarian, casting about for a poster theme, might conceivably take the cue from that casual remark and decide upon a poster featuring "Old Favorites in New Dress," emphasizing the attractive modern editions of the classics now available.

In some junior high school classroom a youngster studying the post-Civil War westward movement, might mention his great-grandmother's sunbonnet, or other souvenir of the period, tucked away in a family trunk in the attic. A poster centering on Pioneer Days would quickly suggest itself to the enterprising teacher. One idea sparks another, and before long a kind of chain reaction has set in. Class discussion is a great stimulus, promoting the sharing of the entire undertaking, and a partnership in the display effort between teacher and pupils.

In the preparation of posters, there are certain fundamentals to observe. Use a poster board that has body, so that it will not buckle or warp. Fourteen ply is generally recommended, except for extra-large display items, when greater thickness is desirable. (Sheet sizes are noted in the Appendix, under Sources of Supplies and Equipment). If tinted board is preferred, choose a color that will not fade. Blue and purple are particularly vulnerable to sunlight.

COLUMBUS DAY

ST. PATRICK'S DAY ❦

GEORGE WASHINGTON

★ ★ ★ ★ ★ ★ ★ ★ ★ ★ ★ ★
ABRAHAM LINCOLN

COLUMBUS DAY

Black old-time lettering for caption, on white cardboard. The style here is "Uncial," and care must be exercised in drawing the letters. The alphabet style is available at public libraries and printing plants

Sussman-Ochs Photo

ST. PATRICK'S DAY

Lettering and shamrocks in bright green, on white. To obtain the old, "eaten-away" look, touch up the outer edges here and there with white dots or thin lines

Sussman-Ochs Photo

GEORGE WASHINGTON

Interesting to do, if time permits. The letters were first painted white, then divided into three equal parts. The upper thirds were then colored red, and the bottoms blue. As an added "patriotic" touch red metallic stars, available at little cost in stationery stores, were pasted in white centers, then the letters were outlined in black

Sussman-Ochs Photo

ABRAHAM LINCOLN

Another lettering style reminiscent of its period, Roman, with peaks in the center on both sides, the letters are black with a black outline. The stars were painted red

Sussman-Ochs Photo

Poster sizes are optional, depending on the space in which they are to be shown, and the amount of material to be used. But if the display area is higher than it is wide, the poster would normally conform. Conversely, if the exhibit area measurements are greater horizontally than vertically, the poster would usually be in accord. Occasionally, for special effect, the procedure would be reversed.

After determining the size and color of the poster, make a rough pencil sketch, indicating wording and placement of caption and design. Avoid clutter. To refer back to "EFFECTIVE LIBRARY EXHIBITS": "Design is an orderly plan of arrangement. It guides the eye from one element to another, with stopping places for emphasis, to a logical climax. The words and illustrations should be grouped and placed in such a way that comprehension is quick and clear. Color masses must be pleasing, well-balanced."

Choose a brief, easy-to-read caption, which conveys at a glance the subject and purpose of the poster. Headings may be hand-lettered, if there is some one at hand with a degree of proficiency in this field, or done with inexpensive cutout letters, in black, white or color, depending upon the preferred background contrast.

LET'S SING AGAIN!

Black lettering on white, with gray staff lines. The clef is a red paper cutout mounted on a vertical rectangle of gray paper

Sussman-Ochs Photo

Let's Sing Again!

CAMPING IS FUN

CAMPING IS FUN

Another novel caption treatment, keeping the subject in mind. Drawn to simulate twigs, the letters were first painted light brown, then dark brown paint was used to shade and highlight them

Sussman-Ochs Photo

LETS LOOK INTO THE FUTURE!!

LET'S LOOK INTO THE FUTURE!

This black-on-white caption is designed to capture attention. The O's and periods for the exclamations are cartoon eyes

Sussman-Ochs Photo

The lettering is an important aspect of poster presentation. Captions should go hand in hand with the art work, and must be planned at the same time, not as an afterthought. Together they make up the poster design, and if correctly controlled, achieve unity and convey the desired message. Sometimes letters alone can do an admirable display "selling" job, as in "Abraham Lincoln," or they can be superimposed on art work to advantage, as in the illustration, Who's Who in the Zoo.

Poster art need not be realistic. Unless the display worker possesses formal art training or genuine talent, attempts at precise drawing are likely to result in unappealing, amateurish creations. Rather, the emphasis should be on large, bold, interesting shapes, easy to execute and strikingly effective, telling the story with a minimum of detail. For the most part the simple, dramatic shapes set the feeling or mood of the poster more successfully than sharply defined drawings.

There are times, however, when strict realism is necessary to put over a point, such as the delineation of various parts of a flower—stamen, sepal, petal, pistil. In this instance drawing ability would be of obvious value. But if the designer cannot draw well, a page from an old nature magazine may suffice.

THE FOURTH OF JULY

An interesting variation. The caption letters were drawn as firecrackers, then painted red. Later the letters were outlined in black

Sussman-Ochs Photo

THE FOURTH OF JULY

THE MERRIE MONTH OF MAY

Materials and Colors
  Ribbon, cardboard, pins, pliers
  Scarlet, pink, yellow, olive green, black, white
Method
  1. Strip of cardboard placed in center of board to represent May pole
  2. Ribbons pinned at top and braided part way down
  3. Ends of ribbons formed into letters and pinned with pliers
  4. Bows at top of pole add to festive mood and finish the design

Sussman-Ochs Photo

WHO'S WHO IN THE ZOO

Materials and Colors
Construction paper, sponge, colored chalk, rubber cement, cardboard
Dark tan, purple, orange, yellow, black, on white
Method
1. Cut rounded edge from full sheets of construction paper
2. Wet paper with sponge, and draw freely lines of the mane in colored chalk
   When paper dries the chalk will not smear
3. Weight paper down while drying, to get it flat
4. Attach the paper to cardboard with rubber cement, double-coated, then all other parts of the poster cut from paper, fastened down in just enough places to secure, but giving a 3-D effect
5. Eyes are printed with circle cut from a soap eraser (art gum) with a razor blade, then dipped in paint

Fred Worthington Photo

Coming into progressively wider use for poster decoration is the so-called "paper sculpture" or cut-out-paper-paste-on technique. Let us imagine that instead of drawing or painting a tree for an Arbor Day poster, a paper silhouette is to be the central figure.

First, with a pencil, outline the shape of a tree on construction paper, and cut out with a pair of sharp scissors. Next, place the tree on the poster board in the position desired, drawing lightly around it. Now remove the tree from the poster board, lay it face down on a piece of newspaper, and coat the back of the cutout with rubber cement. Then similarly coat the area of the poster where the tree is to go, as closely as possible within the pencilled outline (or use the alternative stencil method indicated in the photographs showing the step-by-step handling of tree cutouts). A picture from a discarded magazine could be treated in the same way.

Do not worry about excess cement which has run beyond its boundary. When both cemented areas are tacky, put the construction paper cutout very carefully in proper position, with the bottom line as a guide. At the start, hold a piece of tracing paper between the two cemented areas, and move the tracing paper up as the two make contact. Then smooth the tree onto the entire designated area, using the palm of your hand in an upward stroke, to prevent the formation of air-pockets and bubbles. For added effect cut out tissue paper "leaves," and attach each at one end with the cement, leaving the other end free to flutter as one walks by the poster (see the illustration, Arbor Day). If, by chance, the tree is not in the right place, it can be removed with rubber cement thinner, and then replaced. To do this apply the cement thinner with an eye dropper to one corner of the tree, and pry up with a razor blade or mat knife.

Surplus rubber cement may be rubbed off with another bit of the dried adhesive, called the "pick-up." To get your pick-up, remove a little of the cement clinging to the lip of the dispenser or jar, roll this in your hand until it becomes a ball, and use as you would an eraser where the cement has oozed out from under the glued areas. The same treatment holds for any cement dripping which may have fallen "by mistake" upon other parts of the poster.

PAPER TREE POSTER PROCESS

Decide on size of design and pencil and ruler lightly ma confining lines for area painted

PAPER TREE POSTER PROCES

Turn cutout tree over and r cement entire area, then let

Sussman-Ochs P

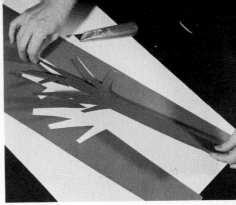

R TREE POSTER PROCESS (2)

Mix paint in large, flat container (top of film can used here). Immerse roller in paint to get it well saturated with color

PAPER TREE POSTER PROCESS (3)

Roll paint on area within pencil lines

PAPER TREE POSTER PROCESS (4

Draw shape of tree, and cut with mat knife

For the present put aside paper from which tree has been removed

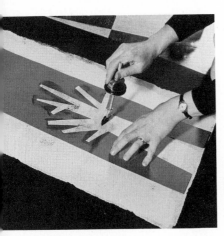

R TREE POSTER PROCESS (6)

Put down paper from which tree shape has been removed, in poster area where tree is to be mounted. (This serves as a stencil, so that little or no cement will get on poster, saving cleanup time later). Now rubber-cement cut out section

PAPER TREE POSTER PROCESS (7)

When both are dry place a sheet of tracing paper between them. Then put tree in proper position over the tracing paper

PAPER TREE POSTER PROCESS (8

Next slowly pull out tracing paper smooth tree down as contact made, with palm of hand

Tree is thus positioned without worrying about getting it stuck in wrong place

PAPER TREE POSTER PROCESS (9)

Cut out leaves from construction paper

PAPER TREE POSTER PROCESS (10

Rubber-cement the leaves onto the tree

Remove any excess adhesive that may have oozed out with "pick-up" — a bit of dried rubber cement

ARBOR DAY, 1962

Materials and Colors
>Construction paper, tissue paper, paint, cardboard
>Light and dark brown, green, black, on white

Method
1. Tissue leaves attached at one end only, to stir as one walks past, or when the air blows them
2. Movement of the leaves creates attention
3. Trees in background denoting young growth printed with edge of cardboard strip dipped in paint

Fred Worthington Photo

Rubber cement is a clear adhesive to be used only when the poster will not come in direct contact for a prolonged period with excessive heat, sunlight or electric light. It is generally an excellent adhering substance for fastening papers and fabrics, for mounting pictures, and performing other functions in connection with poster-making. But it is adversely affected by intense warmth, if subjected to it for a considerable length of time. In such cases plastic glue may be substituted.

Available in gallon cans, rubber cement can also be purchased in smaller glass dispensers with a screw-in brush. It is best applied with a brush. If the cement becomes too thick to handle easily, dilute with rubber cement thinner. For satisfactory results, the cement must be of the consistency for easy spreading.

Smooth poster board is the best surface for cut-out-paper-paste-on (fabric may be substituted for paper) technique, although rough textured board and wood-grain also may be used, if experiments with a small sample show that it will take the pen or brush lines often needed to add realism to the paper presentation.

When a gloss finish is desired for the completed art work, apply a thin coat of rubber cement over the decoration, allow it to dry, then cover with a clear shellac. Another method is to use P.V.A. (Polyvinyl acetate), which eliminates the intermediate steps, or even better, two or three thin coats of Krylon or other spray fixative available in small cans at relatively little cost.

Arresting three-dimensional posters may be produced with surprisingly little trouble. With this thought in mind, build up a supply of papers in assorted textures, patterns and shades, bits of fabric, leather, screening, felt, burlap, and a variety of odds and ends, such as feathers, parts of broken small toys, corks, pipe cleaners, paper doilies, twigs. An empty carton can house the collection.

A feather might inspire a poster on writing, with the "quill" protruding from a cutout paper "ink bottle." The feather, or quill, could be painted, or sprinkled with glitter for added effect. (See illustration, Journey with Genius).

BOOK TREATS FOR BOYS AND GIRLS

Materials and Colors

Construction paper, ink, poster paint, wide paint brush, cardboard, acetate, tissue paper

Strawberry pink, vivid orange, lemon yellow, olive green, purple, black, on white

Method

1. Simple, flat book shapes, pinned away from backdrop
2. Page lines printed with cardboard edge dipped into poster paint
3. Jar drawn, then acetate cut same shape, but slightly smaller, superimposed
4. With wide brush, paint black line around jar and as indicated elsewhere
5. Add brightly colored tissue-paper lollipops, with circles overlapping

Fred Worthington Photo

JOURNEY WITH GENIUS

Materials and cardboard

Cardboard, poster paints, ink, portrait photos of famous people, tissue paper, feather, glue, glitter, paint brush

Blue, purple, magenta, pink, lavender, black, on white

Method

1. Books made of cardboard
2. Paint white thickly on books; while they are still wet, spill ink and lift upper end of poster to let run, giving old marbleized effect to binding
3. Paste portrait photos on spines, or sketch vaguely
4. With thick brush and heavy black poster paint, outline various items shown
5. Flowers made of tissue paper and ink
6. Use real feather, sprinkled first with glue, then glitter

Fred Worthington Photo

ICK AT RANDOM

Materials and Colors

    Tissue paper, rubber cement, cardboard, construction paper, paint

    Pink, white, purple, turquoise, greens, yellow

Method

1. Pattern drawn for tissue paper flower. Several parts cut together, then cemented at one corner. White center binds fastening point, leaving flower petals to sway in the breeze
2. Real book or pamphlet could be used instead of the cardboard and paper version shown

Fred Worthington Photo

A miniature horse from a child's castoff toy might make a decorative or utilitarian figure for a poster design, while the black typewriter ribbon holders might be converted to wheels on a bookish locomotive, if a cardboard cowcatcher and smoke stack are added. (See illustration, Trains).

Searching for interesting things to use, from Alphabet Soup Letters to Zoo Pictures, can make poster work fun.

Many illustrations can be clipped from discarded journals and newspapers, and saved for future use. One of modern advertising's popular practices is to employ photography to advantage, and this medium adapts well to covering with attractive tissue paper for added appeal.

By means of the tissue paper technique and at slight cost, one can obtain a printed color effect that gives a truly professional look to a poster. It can be used when a transparent effect is needed or wanted. (Colored ink serves a similar purpose, but is harder to handle if you are not accustomed to working with a wash).

First the illustration is drawn or laid on the poster board (if the latter, the picture must be pasted smoothly in proper position). Then the tissue paper of the color desired is selected from the roll. Put this directly over the illustration and with a sharp pencil and very light touch, mark the exact outline. Then lift off, and with a pair of scissors, cut as indicated. Now you have the required shape in colored tissue.

Apply a coat of rubber cement, thinned down if necessary, with rubber cement thinner, to the poster illustration. Next, very carefully place the tissue paper cutout within the cemented area. Smooth with your hand, then add another coat of rubber cement over the tissue paper. During this process, work as rapidly as you can. To obtain the most brilliancy from the colored tissue, it is important to get the top coat of cement applied before the undercoat dries.

Ten or twelve minutes later, when the adhesive is as dry as it is likely to get (it tends to stay a bit tacky), cover the entire cemented area with clear shellac. Let this

ROSE TREE PROCESS (Three Illustrations)

Materials and Colors

Tissue paper, flower pots, dowel sticks, styrofoam balls and sheets, pins, needles, thread

Blues, greens, purples, magenta, oranges, pinks, reds—interesting colors, some used as "shading"

Method

1. Cut strips of tissue paper
2. Fold tissue strips over your finger, forming cylinders
3. Tie one end of each cylinder with thread, or sew to hold rose together
4. Put a pin in the closed end, spread the other into the open flower shape, and each rose is ready to be attached
5. Wrap dowel stick with green tissue paper
6. Fill pot with pieces of styrofoam, and "plant" dowel stick, after first sharpening the top end with pencil sharpener or knife
7. Put styrofoam ball on dowel stick (be sure to use ball rightly proportioned to sizes of roses and pots, so as not to get it top-heavy)
8. Press pins into styrofoam ball, following the global contours, clustering roses close together
9. Fill in-between with "leaves" of green tissue, with pins in ends
10. Cover top of pot with tissue, concealing styrofoam

dry thoroughly, to a hard finish. If a brighter gloss seems desirable, cover with another coat of shellac and let dry. This process may be repeated until the treated surface has acquired the appropriate shine or brilliance. A little experimentation in advance, with scrap tissue and board, might be advisable. (Should the display worker prefer, clear spray-can fixative may be used instead of shellac as a final coating for the tissue). The knack will soon be mastered.

If just a protective covering is needed for the art work (rubber cement on top of tissue usually peels), apply only one coat of shellac, and when completely dry to the touch rub the shellacked area with fine steel wool very lightly, being careful not to penetrate the paper surface.

The tissue technique described is also a good way to do a three-color poster while using tissues of only two hues. Overlap makes the difference. After cutting your shapes of color tissue, have them ready to paste, and know where you want the overlap in your illustration to occur. By means of the method explained, put the first shape down, cover with rubber cement, and quickly affix the other color, overlapping it. You will then have a change of color where you have overlapped the tissue, creating the third color. (See illustration, Book Treats for Boys and Girls).

Another effective tissue arrangement is in connection with a photographic collage, combining photographs from discarded magazines. (Of course, it goes without saying that pictures or prints that must be returned, or used again, are not to be considered, for this process is permanent). After the poster board is organized with a well-designed layout of photographs which have been attached by means of a thin coat of rubber cement, the tissue paper can be applied in the order previously indicated:

1. Rubber cement over pictures
2. Colored tissue paper added
3. Rubber cement coating
4. Shellac after drying

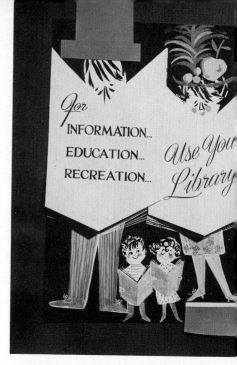

FOR INFORMATION, EDUCATION, RECREATION, USE YOUR LIBRARY

Materials and Colors
Cardboard, construction paper, p...
ink
Method
1. Figures were first painted in w...
on blackboard, then ink was...
plied over white in bright colors

Note: See related comment in this chapt...

ANOTHER SERVICE, NEWSPAPER COLLECTION

(See related comment, this chapter)

BOOK WEEK

BOOKS FOR BUSINESS MEN

A special exhibit, joining cardboard panels in mustard color, flash pink, golden yellow and tangerine, to back up a book exhibit for a meeting of Baltimore's Rotary Club.
Designed, and in large part prepared by Emily Hagan, of the Enoch Pratt Free Library

Sussman-Ochs Photos

EXECUTIVES IN ACTION

Reverse of foregoing backdrop, with actual titles lettered on spines of the drawn books

The overlay of color welds the photographs into a unit, and brightens an otherwise sombre array. More than one color may be applied to the photograph collage, if desired. In fact, two or three colors, each covering its own portion of the arrangement, would be more effective. Since the tissue is transparent, the photographs are easily seen. For this type of effort the poster caption should be done in black bold letters, with the tissue paper put on quickly, so that the message will appear clear and conspicuous through the color. Or else the letters may be mounted on the tissue, contrasting well with the bright colors.

Tissue paper can also be used as a three-dimensional form, particularly in the production of pleasing and life-like flowers. Yellow tissue paper may be folded and cut into daisy-type petal shapes (by proper folding, many petals can be produced at the same time). These petals should be glued to a circle of thin cardboard or heavy construction paper. Snip out a stem and leaves from construction paper or cardboard, and for the finishing touch either crayon or paint dots in the center of the cardboard circle, for each "daisy." (See illustration, Pick at Random).

To fashion the flowers for a rose tree, wind pieces of folded tissue paper over your fingers, forming cylinders, then tie one end of each with thread. Next put a pin in the closed end, spread the other into the open flower shape, and each "rose" is ready to be attached. (See photographs of a rose tree in process).

CAPTURE SUMMER MAGIC THROUGH BOOKS

Materials and Colors

    Cardboard, masking tape, sponge, ink, tissu
paper

    Purple, blue, green, black

Method

1. Center background effect achieved by pour
   ing purple, blue and pale green ink o
   large sponge, and pushing this acros
   board
2. Side panels added with masking tape. (Thi
   screen was made to hide an unattractive air
   conditioner)
3. Each butterfly cut from white paper, wit
   tissue duplicate applied over it, then painte
   with ink
4. The net was made of black lines printe
   with edge of cardboard strip; books on sid
   panels treated the same way

Fred Worthington Phot

White poster board is recommended when work-ing with the tissue paper technique, as the colors do not come through strongly on tinted board. The best results with tissue paper can be obtained through experimenting in the medium. There is virtually no end to the striking effects that can be achieved through bold, bright shapes of color in poster innovations. (The illustration, Religious Books, is one example).

Bear constantly in mind that poster work must be clearly visible across the room or hall. The original art need not be restricted to one treatment or technique, but may offer a combination of several, for greater impact. If, for instance, a thick, dark line is necessary to set off a figure properly, and more delicate treatment is re-quired for the face, use a heavy crayon line or a fairly heavy brush with poster paint for the former, and a thin crayon or pencil line for the latter. (See illustration, Reading for Fun).

When poster art requires joining two or more pieces of paper, fabric or cardboard, use masking tape

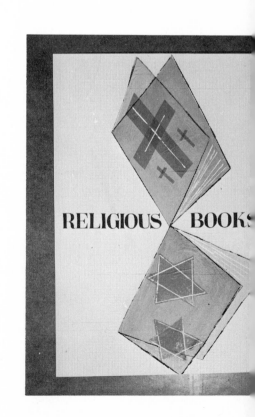

RELIGIOUS BOOKS

READING FOR FUN

Materials and Colors·
Cardboard, construction paper, tracing paper, crayon, ink, pictures cut from old magazines no longer needed

Green, blue, red orange, orange, black, on white

Method
1. Cut letters and place them
2. Draw figure on tracing paper, blacken back of tracing paper, then trace on board in proper position
3. Go over lines with black crayon
4. With large brush flooded with ink, freely apply color inside of lines, and the few areas outside of lines, as shown. (Practice with flooded brush on scrap board first)
5. Next apply book, with pictures from a discarded magazine, if available. A book may be substituted for the above, if preferred

Fred Worthington Photo

US BOOKS

erials and Colors
Cardboard, paint, ink, tissue paper, rubber cement
Pink orange, purple, blue, black, on white
od
1. Books end to end provide good design area for lettering
2. Books covered with tissue paper
3. Black, white lines printed with edge of cardboard dipped in paint

Fred Worthington Photo

on the underside, with colored adhesive cloth tape on the top side, to make the seams as inconspicuous as possible. If a seam is quite evident despite your best efforts, then turn it into an advantage, by making the added area more decorative (see illustrations Capture Summer Magic through Books and Books for Business Men). Transparent adhesive tape is seldom suitable for such work, because it has a tendency to dry out after a time, turns yellow and detracts from the favorable appearance. Of course, when an amber or yellowing effect is needed to add color interest, or an antique finish, the transparent tape is an asset.

In the interest of economy, posters may be reused at intervals, in whole or in part. Originally the poster, For Information, Education, Recreation, Use Your Library, was part of an exhibit representing a family reading together. When this display was dismantled, the poster was carefully wrapped, labeled and stored. Later, when a small Book Week display was needed, the poster was brought out, cut at the logical point (in this case, in half) and converted to the Book Week poster illustrated. The

remaining portion was turned into the poster titled Another Service, Newspaper Collection, by pasting on a piece of newsprint cut into the desired shape.

For mounting posters, use small steel pins in the corners, touching up the pinheads with matching paint. A cardboard border in contrasting color often sets off the poster effectively, or narrow cardboard strips, placed horizontally or vertically, may do likewise. When the poster is done, be sure to remove fingerprints and pencil marks, with a pink pearl eraser or a piece of art gum. Neatness is essential in all kinds of display work, for maximum attention.

The life of a poster may sometimes be prolonged by use of Krylon, or other fixative. When handling is a hazard to delicate colors, or the colors are in danger of rubbing off, a fixative may be sprayed on. This is a colorless varnish that gives added protection. But its application means a gloss finish, which some people may find objectionable.

Another type of preservative is the plasticized sheeting, Permafilm, obtainable in the 50 ft. roll, 24 inches wide. A piece slightly larger than the size of the poster is cut. This is laid carefully over the poster, smoothed flat from top to bottom as pressure is applied with the hand, in sweeping motion, to avoid bubbles between the adhering paper and the cardboard or other poster surface. Then the edges are neatly trimmed, securing the covering and making the piece both airtight and waterproof. In cutting Permafilm the required size, be sure to leave one corner of the roll remaining freely separated, otherwise it will be hard to get started again.

TRAINS

Materials and Colors

Multi-color book jackets, constru͏ paper, cardboard, tissue paper, e͏ reels from typewriter ribbons, paint͏ ton tape, upholstery tacks, scissors,͏ Black, pink, violet, blue, on white

Method

1. Stuff book jackets with dummy b͏ (discards, or other volumes no l͏ needed)
2. To attach each book to bu͏ board,* "insert narrow cotton tap͏ tween the paper jacket and͏ cover, knotting ends at center͏ Then below and above the kno͏ sert two upholstery tacks, pu͏ through the tape with points f͏ out. Snip off tape ends with sc͏ and press the books into the de͏ position, the points penetrating͏ backdrop. Two long pins placed͏ neath each book will keep it͏ sagging to right or left."
3. Face cut from construction p͏ features painted on in white, wit͏ sue of bright pink for cheeks and͏ for eyes pasted over the white
4. Smokestack and cowcatcher, ͏ cardboard
5. Smoke is tissue cut and pinned,͏ color atop the other
6. Typewriter ribbon reels used͏ wheels, pinned on, with small sq͏ of cardboard as "washers"

*From "Effective Library Exhibits," pag͏

Sussman-Ochs

CHAPTER FOUR / ATTENTION-GETTING BULLETIN BOARDS

The finest diamond in the world, if placed in a tawdry brass setting, would inevitably lose much of its luster. But suitably mounted, the stone's flashing beauty is greatly enhanced and properly appreciated.

Even the most attractive display piece, when affixed to an ugly, pockmarked bulletin board, will fail to make the most of its potential drawing power. However, set against a fitting background, it instantly becomes a compelling eye-catching device, serving as an effective advocate of the subject being projected.

To the novice, a bare bulletin board of even moderate size, prominently located in library or classroom, looks at least as large as the Grand Canyon. The responsibility is there. What to do about it?

First decide on the subject to be featured. Then select a caption that is short, appealing and thought-provoking. A good caption is the key to a successful bulletin board, since it must tell at a glance what the display is about, and at the same time arouse the curiosity and interest of viewers.

Keeping the proportions of the bulletin board in mind, as in the case of the poster, make a rough pencil sketch indicating color treatment and approximate placement of items which will best carry out your plan.

A fresh coat of quick-drying casein paint, easily applied, can frequently rejuvenate an old, badly soiled cork bulletin board. Sometimes even a good scrubbing will do the trick. For a more ambitious effort, line the bulletin board with large sheets of colored construction paper or cardboard. Similarly, wallpaper of appropriate design, often available free for the asking in leftover rolls, may provide pleasing color contrast as well as a

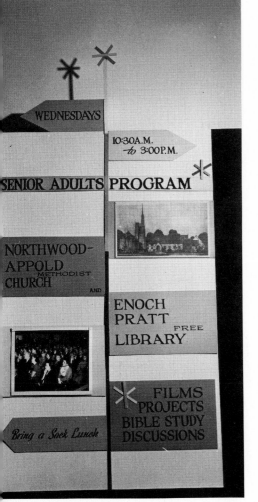

SENIOR ADULTS PROGRAM
Branch, Enoch Pratt Free Library

Materials and Colors
    Cardboard, photographs, construction paper, ink
    Golden yellow, yellow, orange, olive green, black
Method
    1. Display extended above bulletin board for added interest
    2. Asterisk, or star on top adds "fun" touch to the project

Fred Worthington Photo

LISTEN TO STORY HOUR

Materials and Colors
> Cardboard, ink, brush, printed fabric, felt-tip pen, ruler
> White, pink, orange, yellow

Method
1. Figure drawn on wrong side of white cardboard, and cut out with mat knife (this eliminated drawing first on tracing paper and then transferring to white cardboard)
2. Features, shoes, and hair done with brush and ink
3. Fabric cut for dress
4. Books cut from cardboard in deeper variations of dress colors
5. Lines for pages drawn with felt-tip pen and ruler

Sussman-Ochs Photo

clean, fresh setting. Inexpensive fabrics, corrugated paper, burlap, felt, peg board, linoleum remnants, make attractive mounts. Sheets of metallic paper and holiday gift wrappings, carefully chosen, can add a festive air.

If your bulletin board is vertical, evolve a vertical pattern, depending on arresting color combinations and arrangement of materials to attract attention. A horizontal bulletin board calls for a horizontal pattern, with the display materials strategically distributed across its width. Guard against overcrowding, which gives the impression of a "too busy" board. Regardless of the variation in size, shape and height of individual display items and groups of items, the overall composition must present a unified appearance.

Interesting bulletin board designs may be developed with the addition of strips, rectangles, squares, triangles and circles, effective for mounting purposes, or for supplementary decoration. Cut from paper or cardboard obtainable in a profusion of appealing shades, these dress up a bulletin board so that the poster and its accompanying display materials may be presented to the best advantage. Engaging arrangements can be achieved either by formal balance, or by varying the grouping of materials at different levels and angles, thereby creating an off-balance pattern that is unified, but agreeable to look at. The latter method is preferable, as the consistent use of symmetrical designs tends toward monotony.

Invariably the strips, rectangles, squares or other design elements should be arranged in such a way as to lead the viewers' eyes straight to the target area—the poster and other important display items. The patterns may range in treatment from traditional to modern, de-

camera

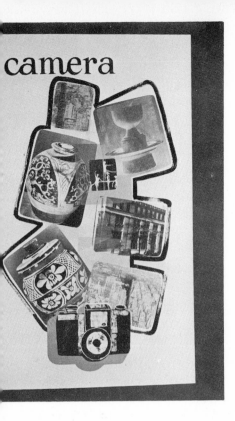

CAMERA

Materials and Colors
   Photostats, tissue, shellac, cardboard
   Gray, orange, yellow, hot pink, yellow green,
   black, pale olive, on white board
Method
   1. Photostats are covered with tissue paper and
      shellac
   2. Camera drawn, cut out of cardboard, and
      pinned with a ½" thick piece of wallboard
      behind it, to give 3-D effect

Fred Worthington Photo

pending on the theme and mood of the display. A highly stylized poster dealing with contemporary architecture, if serving as the principal lure, would demand modern supplementary decoration. On the other hand, a poster illustrating American life in Colonial times, would naturally call for a background more in keeping with that period. Repetition of the motif is often effective, especially on horizontal bulletin boards. The pattern figures can be identically traced, or slightly changed each time. (See illustration, Bringing Books As Gifts).

As indicated above, the exhibit's subject matter has important bearing on the type of treatment advisable. If the theme-setting poster relates to "Heroes of History" or "American Industry," the remaining decoration would be relatively strong and bold. Feminine fashions, jewelry, chinaware, flowers or cookery would suggest a lighter, more delicate approach.

It goes without saying that the background must be subordinate to the main display. Since its principal purpose is to set off and point up the chief exhibit elements, it should never be allowed to become the dominating factor, drawing attention away from the major attractions. Obviously, then, to fulfill its function successfully, the background must strengthen, not weaken, the primary exhibit. (Note illustration, Books They Talk about on the Party Line).

The whole bulletin board arrangement stems from and ties in with the caption, or heading. Bulletin board captions must be large enough to be seen from a distance, and should contain familiar, easy-to-read words in lettering styles pleasing to their audience. Obviously, the childish lowercase manuscript letters suitable for youngsters in the primary grades, would hardly be appropriate for teen-age or adult displays. There is a wide

RTHER VARIETY
IN CAPTION TREATMENT

BOATING—Spelled out with rope, stiffened with starch

HOLIDAYS — Cardboard cutout, brushed with glue, and glitter sprinkled on

SPRING—Drawn on cardboard strip, glue brushed on, and miniature flowers superimposed

man-Ochs Photos

WINTER—Wool yarn pasted on cardboard, then "snowflakes" from paper doilies added

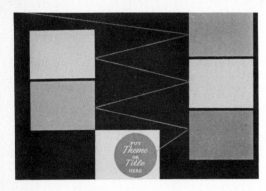

BULLETIN BOARD DESIGNS

For mounting pictorial, printed or written matter
Yellow, pink, tangerine, golden yellow, rose, on black

Method
1. Cardboard rectangles of same size arranged in pleasing color pattern, and tied together with orange wool
2. In the smaller design the title may be lettered in white on a red cardboard circle mounted on a white cardboard rectangle
3. The larger board may have the title in black, on a white circle

Sussman-Ochs Photos

diversity in cutout commercial alphabets available at little cost, both individually and in printers' fonts, with the proper assortment of vowels and consonants. Many of these are listed in the Appendix. Or, if a Cutawl machine or jigsaw is available, they may be cut from cardboard, styrofoam, or wallboard, after the letter patterns have been drawn on brown wrapping paper. Hand-cut paper letters, if skilfully done, are acceptable, but this is a time-consuming process.

Hand-lettered captions, if well executed, are also effective, especially when placed on attractive background strips in contrasting color. For variety, interesting captions may be spelled out with heavy cord, rope, raffia, narrow metallic or silk ribbon, or colored cotton tape. For emphasis, some words may be stiffened by dipping in starch or poster paints.

Unusual effects for special displays can be obtained by writing the caption in plastic glue upon cardboard, paper or fabric strips, then sprinkling on glitter (liquid glitter is also now available), confetti, gravel, sand, etc. For a bulletin board on SPRING, apply tiny artificial flowers to this glue-spelled word. Miniature leaves could be used for AUTUMN, while "snow," "snowflakes" or "icicles" cut from paper doilies or obtainable in display supply stores, could be applied to the wet glue for WINTER. (For additional references to lettering, consult "HOW-TO" HELPS).

To assure that cutout caption letters are straight, pin a thin wooden strip or cardboard guide-line onto the bulletin board temporarily. Spacing between letters and words must be uniform, bottoms properly aligned. Measure when necessary. Uneven spacing gives a ragged, unprofessional look.

When mounting pictures, maps, book jackets, students' papers or three-dimensional objects on a bulletin board, neatness of attachment is imperative. Annotated labels, nicely hand-lettered in black ink or show-

HIGH SCHOOL EXHIBIT, Baltimore
Photo by Hecker Portraits

UNESCO EXHIBIT
Denver Public Library
Photo by Bob Schott

card color, or clearly typed, should appear with any items requiring explanation or identification. Avoid the use of large steel or brass thumb tacks, conspicuous nails or clips, botchy paste-up jobs when mounting, for these detract greatly from the general appearance. Measure for straightness of line and evenness of balance, or contrived unbalance. When pins or tacks are used, touch up the heads with paints to match surrounding color areas. Care must be taken to keep the means of attachment as unobtrusive as possible. In the Appendix, under SOURCES OF SUPPLIES AND EQUIPMENT, may be found a variety of suggestions for mounting materials.

The tissue paper technique mentioned in the foregoing chapter may be adapted to bulletin boards, as well. For example, newspaper and magazine clippings, or student papers, can be set against background silhouettes in eye-catching color, relating to the subject featured.

When stressing current events, items dealing with countries in the news might be mounted on tissue map silhouettes. Clippings pertaining to food and nutrition might be affixed to a large, bright tissue paper salad bowl, while those dealing with animal pets could be superimposed on dog, cat or other animal silhouettes. Construction paper shadow shapes are also effective, or a combination of both types of paper could be used.

Overlaying tissue paper as part of the bulletin board decoration can be an exciting color experience because of the transformation in tones when the covering occurs. Against a white background tissue paper circles, rectangles, triangles, or more imaginative shapes

BRINGING BOOKS AS GIFTS

can be cut either with precision or without, and arranged to overlap or stand free, as one "plays around" with the design until the results are completely satisfying.

As in the case of posters, a photographic collage from discarded magazines can be prepared for bulletin board use with tissue paper as an overlay of color, unifying the different-sized pictures chosen to represent the theme. (See illustrations, Camera and Our Yesterdays).

The overall selection of color is exceedingly important. Harmony and/or contrast must be employed strategically for the greatest benefit to the composition. If the principal display elements are light, a dark background with light accents may be in order. When dark colors predominate in the main exhibit areas, a light background with dark accents is indicated. Which arrangement is likely to gain the greatest attention and create the most favorable, lasting impression? In the final analysis, the answer to this question must be the determining factor.

BRINGING BOOKS AS GIFTS
(Children's display, Enoch Pratt Free Library)

Materials and Colors
Construction paper, cardboard, real pine greens, tiny Christmas balls and figures, string, felt-tip pen, paint, ink, book jackets
Green, yellow, orange, red, purple, pink, on white

Method
1. Hair made from paper ends from print shop, curled and braided
2. Long, straight hair, paper cut into thin strips
3. Real pine greens decorated with miniature Christmas balls and figures
4. Construction paper cut very thin and tied in bows at girls' necks
5. Black lines around all figures done with felt-tip pen

Sussman-Ochs Photo

OUR YESTERDAYS

Materials and Colors
Tissue paper, book jackets, photographs or photostats
Purple, blue, olive, magenta, on white

Method
1. Using tissue paper technique, make background shapes of color for book jackets
2. Photographs are also covered with tissue. (In this case photostats were made of photos in an old book, no longer copyrighted). The negatives were also used on strips to coordinate the display—the large one for case backdrop, small ones for shelf signs)

Fred Worthington Photo

OUR CITY — AND HOW IT GROWS

Materials and Colors
> Cardboard, wood, tissue paper, twigs, thumb tacks, construction paper, crayon
> Red, magenta, yellow orange, red orange, white, black, on navy blue

Method
1. Baltimore's famous "white stone steps" made from wood, painted white, and glued to backdrop
2. Cardboard used for "houses" and "doors"
3. Bent construction paper forms fence
4. Twigs used for trees, tissue paper leaves cut and glued on
5. Finishing touches in black paint, printed with edge of cardboard, and crayon
6. Letters painted on

Note: This display sat on a shelf at the Enoch Pratt Free Library, where books about Baltimore were displayed. It could also be attached to a bulletin board, or would stand free if a piece of cardboard were taped on for a "floor."

Sussman-Ochs Photo

"CURIOUS GEORGE"
Branch display, The Enoch Pratt Free Library

Materials and Colors
> Cardboard, bright-colored patterned paper, textured paper, felt, string, plastic balls, paint
> Yellows, pinks, blue-greens, black and white

Method
1. "Curious George," the popular juvenile storybook character created by H. A. Rey, was cut from wallboard, and covered with textured paper
2. Ears and feet made of felt
3. "Balloons" were made from plastic colored balls from the dime store, cut in half and pinned over patterned paper circles in bright colors, which showed through the plastic

Sussman-Ochs Photo

.K MUSIC

Materials and Colors

Construction paper, cardboard, pins, paint, roller, masking tape

Red, white, black, blue

Method

1. Hair cut from construction paper into a coil, projects to form shadows when pinned down
2. Accordion cut from cardboard put together with masking tape and pinned away (accordion fashion) from background
3. Sweater rolled on with paint roller, and rough edges look "natural"
4. Handles and hands added
5. Scarf of construction paper

"MADELINE"

Material and Colors

Cloth, doily, ribbon, paint, rope, wallboard, buttons, mat knife, construction paper, pins, cardboard

Pale oranges, yellows, blues, black, white

Method

1. Figure blown up from the popular children's books by Bemelmans, and cut from wallboard with Cutawl machine
2. Madeline dressed in cloth, doily, ribbon, paint
3. Rope is painted to color and stiffen hair, which is pinned on
4. Cloth and buttons pinned on
5. Buildings drawn on cardboard and cut with mat knife
6. Trees cut from construction paper

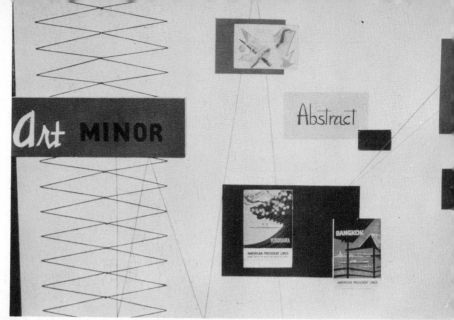

ART MINOR

Another modern design, achieved with simple materials and good contrast, at the secondary level of Baltimore's public schools

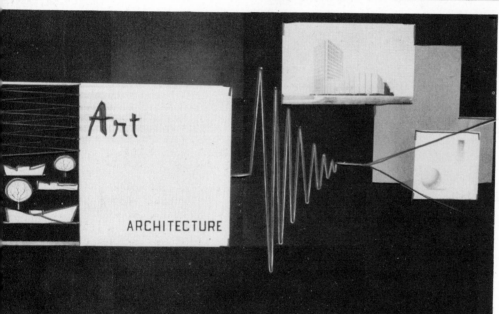

ART, ARCHITECTURE

An interesting modern arrangement with board and yarn of constrasting colors, set up in a Baltimore public high school

RECESSED DISPLAY

The Brooklyn Public Library

FOR BOOKS ON TRAINING AND SUPERVISION

Materials and Method

Drawing board, clip board, and other objects in this display were cut from 14-ply colored cardboard. An actual blueprint was rubber-cemented to a piece of cardboard and thumb-tacked into position. Thumb tacks were also used on the T Square. The main heading and book titles were hand-lettered. Lines on clip board pages were ruled in with pen and colored ink, and the mathematical formulas done with heavy crayon. Some of the items are given dimension by pinning away from board over small pieces of insulite (wallboard), and the entire display is mounted on the backdrop by means of long steel pins which are bent over on the back of the cardboard and anchored by pieces of masking tape

Artist, Emily Hagan
Sussman-Ochs Photo

CHILDREN'S READING ROOM DECORATION

Materials and Colors

Cardboard, felt-tip pen, paint, ink, paper

Pale shades of blue, green, yellow, tan, purple, pink, orange, on white, with accents of black—blending well with the interior of the Enoch Pratt Free Library's Dundalk Avenue Branch, where it was installed

Method

1. Enlarged cardboard books, cut at angles to look opened, have "pages" indicated by felt-tip pen and ruler
2. The books, given dimension by concealed blocks of wallboard, are glued and pinned to backdrop, for added security
3. The pictures—relating youngsters to the four seasons, are self-explanatory, requiring no caption

Sussman-Ochs Photo

EXHIBIT HONORING THE 50TH ANNIVERSARY OF THE ANTIQUE AUTOMOBILE CLUB OF AMERICA

The Free Library of Philadelphia

"An opaque projector enlarged the old Philadelphia prints on white no-seam paper, and the artist followed the outline with a rough black stroke. The little antique cars were made out of wallboard and were painted in full color. They were attached to the background by means of pegs so that they appeared to be rolling along the street parallel to the facade of the buildings"

FOLK MUSIC DISPLAY,
Denver Public Library

"Exhibit on floor peg board to announce opening of the Folk Music collection . . . Background of light blue paper with white cutout instruments and colorful Peter Hunt-type drawings"

Exhibit by Janice White

Photo by Bob Gordon

JUVENILE EXHIBIT
The Brooklyn Public Library

RELIGIOUS EXHIBIT
The Brooklyn Public Library

MEMORIAL EXHIBIT
The Brooklyn Public Library

Friends of the Library project

Photo by Christensen and Boesen

57

CHILDREN'S POSTER
Glendale Public Library
"Boy and Rocking Horse in color
paper sculpture, with hand-lette
ing"

Display artist, Eloise M. Fre

OUR SUMMER TRAIN TRIP

Materials and Colors
Black paper, chalk, construction paper, straw place mats,
straw coasters, paper clips,
pins, angora yarn, paint
White, pink, yellow, red, red
orange
Method
1. Cover bulletin board with
   black paper
2. Draw track lines with chalk
3. Sun is circle cut from paper
   in bright colors
4. Train is made of straw
   place mats (this gives a
   summery look, and goes
   along with caption)
5. Wheels are straw coasters
6. Paper clips used for train
   couplings
7. Smoke drawn on with
   chalk, then angora yarn
   pinned over smoke lines

Sussman-Ochs Photo

FOREIGN AFFAIRS BULLETIN BOARD, in a Baltimore high school

Photo by Hecker Portraits

COMMEMORATIVE EXHIBIT
The Brooklyn Public Library

Honoring the seventy-fifth anniversary of the Civil Service merit system in New York State

OUR CITY AND HOW IT GROWS

NOTE: Same as display (prepared for fall showing), with Christmas decorations added in December

Sussman-Ochs Photo

HISTORICAL EXHIBIT
The Brooklyn Public Library

LIBRARY FAMILY WEEK

JUNE 18 THROUGH 24

TAKE ALONG SOME BOOKS FROM THE CHILDREN'S DEPARTMENT

LIBRARY FAMILY WEEK

A display arranged at Baltimore's Eno[ch] Pratt Free Library, with cardboard c[ut] outs designed by Emily Hagan

To get the printed effect, "Baltim[ore Families Read," across the op[en] pages of the book, type was s[et] and repeated, one line under t[he] other, to fill an entire sheet. Enou[gh] type proofs were then run off [to] form the pages. The pages we[re] cut out of white cardboard a[nd] then rubber-cemented in positi[on] and trimmed to fit. Both the hea[ds] and book were cut out of two col[ors] of cardboard with the Cutawl m[a]chine, and the entire display w[as] mounted on a piece of wallboar[d.] Some of the figures were pinn[ed] away from the backdrop, to gi[ve] dimension

Sussman-Ochs Ph[oto]

FIRE PREVENTION WEEK

Materials and Colors
    Tissue paper, rubber cement, cutout letters, gold paper or cardboard, chalk, ruler
    Magenta, red, orange, white, pale gray, on black
Method
    1. Tissue paper "fire"—crumpled a bit to create shadows in the light. Attached with rubber cement
    2. Graduated letters in white cut out
    3. Nozzle of hose cut from gold cardboard, or cardboard covered with metallic gold paper
    4. Wet chalk-drawn lines drawn for light beam, with ruler or thin stick as guide

Fred Worthington Photo

FIRE PREVENTION WEEK

CHAPTER FIVE / CLASSROOM PRACTICES

There are two major views in so far as classroom bulletin boards are concerned. One maintains that they must be showcases for students' work, with the youngsters themselves largely responsible for both content and presentation. The use by the teacher of posters and designs suggested or originating elsewhere is frowned upon, even though this might mean a vastly improved representation.

The second view—with which this writer is in hearty accord—argues that the teacher, because of his broad experience and training, should provide most of the ideas and leadership, democratically inviting student participation, and using student work wherever practicable.

However, if he is by talent or temperament artistically inadequate, he may legitimately borrow ideas, materials and/or techniques from any available source, in order to make classroom bulletin boards brighter, more attractive, more potentially educative. Certainly it is not plagiarism, but justifiable resourcefulness to adapt existing tools tending to stimulate learning, or to assist more readily in the dissemination of information.

Where would the world be today if the great scientists, inventors, explorers, historians and medical researchers had ignored earlier developments in their respective fields, or failed to take into account the findings and accomplishments of their predecessors and contemporaries? Surely in teaching, as in other areas, there is the obligation to seize upon any constructive means likely to further the desired goals.

James B. League, an enthusiastic and capable young teacher in Baltimore's elementary schools, has created many successful classroom bulletin board dis-

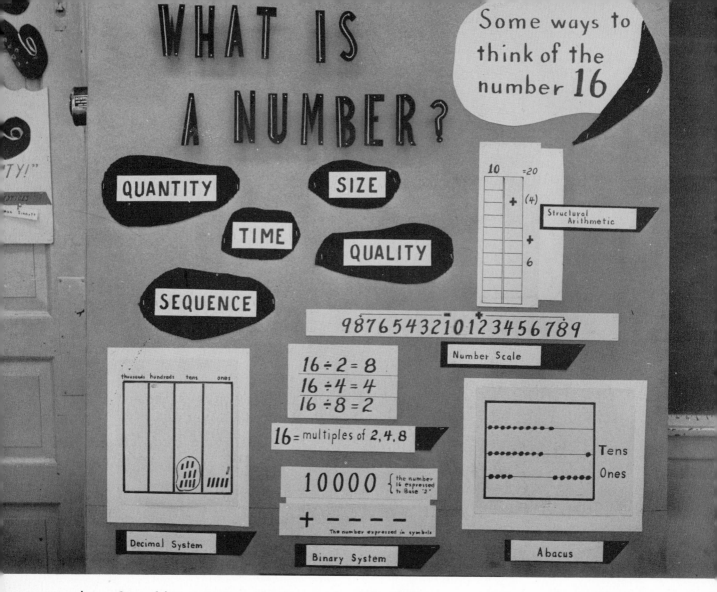

Some ways to think of the number 16

WHAT IS A NUMBER?

QUANTITY   SIZE

TIME   QUALITY

SEQUENCE

Structural Arithmetic

$10 \quad =20$
$+ \ (4)$
$+ \ 6$

$9\,8\,7\,6\,5\,4\,3\,2\,1\,0\,1\,2\,3\,4\,5\,6\,7\,8\,9$

Number Scale

thousands hundreds tens ones

$16 \div 2 = 8$
$16 \div 4 = 4$
$16 \div 8 = 2$

$16 =$ multiples of $2, 4, 8$

Tens
Ones

10000 { the number 16 expressed in Base "2"

$+ \ - \ - \ - \ -$

The number expressed in symbols

Decimal System

Binary System

Abacus

---

plays. Out of his experience he has evolved the following philosophy:

"In order to proceed with maximum understanding it seems necessary to outline certain objectives or goals to be desired of visual materials. Without this statement, one flounders in confusion. The statement of objectives is also necessary from the point of view of establishing sub-goals to be used as means of arriving at the final goals. All material included in this statement is developed from my own classroom teaching experience, and is stated from my personal viewpoint only.

"1. **Objectives**

1. To create the maximum aesthetic 'value' with the abilities and materials available to each teacher

2. To create visual displays that have mind-appeal as well as eye-appeal

3. To provide high standards of visual display to serve as a basis of experience for children to develop their own background and eventually their own skills in this area

WHAT IS A NUMBER?

A classroom bulletin board in Baltimo
for an Intermediate Grade
Materials
1. Plain cork backdrop
2. Black corrugated paper
3. Construction paper
4. Heavy gauge pins
Methods and Colors
1. The captions were yellow contrasting background
2. The examples were on gr mounted on yellow
3. The five kinds of numbers we on yellow, mounted on fr forms of black corrugat paper
4. The letters were mounted 2" pins to stand away fr the board
Children's Participation
1. Helped assemble materi and assisted in putting up

Sussman-Ochs Ph

Sussman-Ochs Photo

FE LONG AGO

A classroom bulletin board in Baltimore, for an Intermediate Grade

Materials
1. Dark blue-green burlap for background; painted palm fronds; metallic green dinosaur; blue, blue-green and green tissue paper; yarn; construction paper; flat pictures

Colors and Methods
1. Blue-green, greens and blues
2. The tissue paper was crumpled to suggest wild growth and water, the metallic paper dinosaur was placed to "feed" on the painted palm fronds

Children's Participation
1. Helped assemble materials and put up

4. To develop the teacher's outlook to a point where he is sensitive to many ideas as potential points of departure for display or visual set-ups
5. To remember that fundamentally visual material should be, after all, an integral part of the educative processes, and therefore a primary responsibility of the teacher, himself

"The following list of points serves to establish some reasons why it can be argued that the teacher needs to take the dominant role in planning, preparation, and execution of visual materials. (This is counter to the position that children should perform this function, and the teacher take a rather subordinate role, because schools are more interested in developing healthy personalities than beautiful art products).

"1. The preparation of quality displays requires a perception and/or appreciation of several factors, among which are:

a. an intellectual awareness of the salient points of the topic or subject to be displayed . . . i.e., how to create and capitalize on clever captions and related materials such as pictures, books, mock-ups, etc.

b. a sensitivity to certain principles of color and design as adjuncts of the message to be conveyed

c. the ability to gauge the viewers' reaction— e.g., appropriate materials for age and/or mentality groups

"2. The final display should be more than a sum of its parts (i.e., color, design, caption, etc.). Rather, it should possess an organic unity which is the end product of intelligent planning

"3. The display should have 'sales' value as well as aesthetic value. It is the teacher who understands fully the message (however subtle or bold) he wishes to have communicated by the display materials

"4. In the final analysis, it is the teacher who must grow in experience and skill in the development of effective displays. He will need to use these skills at a high level of efficiency for many years to come. The sense of design, and 'healthy personality' can be developed in children in countless other ways

"5. The teacher, himself, needs to develop a forward look to keep his displays stimulating, and at the aforementioned high level of efficiency of execution

"Certainly I do not advocate leaving the children out of the picture. That is not my intention at all. I should like to make these additional points, and a more resourceful teacher could probably come up with many others:

ROOM DECORATION

To improve the appearance of an unattractive corner of a Fifth Grade classroom in Baltimore, the teacher mounted some children's art papers on walls and cabinets, placing artistic objects nearby. With the colors nicely coordinated, the arrangement made a pleasant reading corner

Sussman-Ochs Photo

"1. In order to help the children to develop good display principles, one bulletin board in the room can be turned over to them. This could be done on a monthly rotating committee basis, four or five boys and girls working together. Such a setup would give all the children experience during the year in the planning and execution of exhibits. Being responsible for a single board, and knowing what was expected of them, they would probably feel more secure

"2. Because the teacher, in a sense, takes the dominant role, does not mean that the children are excluded during the preparation and execution activities. They could be included in various ways: Designing and cutting letters from folded squares of construction paper, if no commercial alphabets are available

Dismantling previous displays

Preparing the backgrounds for new displays, by painting or lining

Helping in choice of pictures in planning stage

Assisting with mounting of pictures, maps, charts or other items

Getting books from library when these are to be used

Putting jackets on books

Filing dismantled materials for future use

Lending material from their personal collections—shells, stamps, baseball cards, rock specimens, etc.

"3. Children, quite naturally from a maturational point of view, lack the sensitivity and intellectual awareness to prepare displays with the necessary depth of understanding to carry a teaching message effectively

"4. Finally, children themselves love to see their own creative products displayed to best advantage"

WALL EXHIBIT

A Baltimore School with little or no display space made use of classroom walls for mounting children's work

Sussman-Ochs Photo

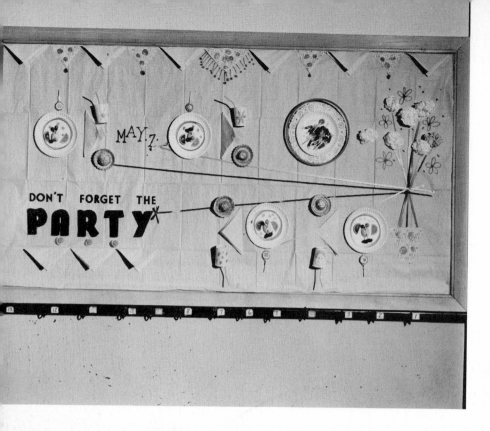

DON'T FORGET THE PARTY

Materials and Colors

Dime store paper party goods—
table cloth, napkins, plates, cups
straws; paper doily; bright-colored miniature Mexican hats
candy and lollipops; facial tissues
patterned wrapping paper; satin
ribbon; pins, construction paper,
ink, paint

Multi-colors

Method

1. Table cloth, napkins, cups,
   straws, set as for a party
2. Doily and hats add to party
   feeling
3. Real candy and gay lollipops
   glued and pinned to plates and
   table
4. 3-D flowers made from facial
   tissue, on paper stems, set into
   pot cut from patterned wrapping paper
5. Satin ribbon pulls eye from
   decorations to flowers to lettered message, unifying the
   composition on the large bulletin board

Sussman-Ochs Photo

KINDERGARTEN ACTIVITIES

Materials and Colors

Cover paper, string, cardboard, construction paper,
ink, paints

Red, blue, yellow, green,
black, on white

Method

1. Figures, clothes, cut from
   construction paper
2. Fringed paper for eye-
   lashes
3. Books, blocks, beads, jigsaw puzzle, apparel de-
   tails, made from construction paper
4. Various items in the composition pinned away from
   backdrop, to give 3-D effect

Fred Worthington Photo

GOOD BOOKS ARE TREASURES

Done by Fifth Graders in Baltimore

Sussman-Ochs Photo

STRENGTHENING OUR GOVERNMENT

Done by 11th Grade students, Baltimore County Public Schools

SOCIAL STUDIES BULLETIN BOARDS

Organized and prepared by Senior High School Students of Baltimore County Public Schools, Grades 10 through 12

REGIONS OF THE U.S.A.

A classroom bulletin board arranged for an Intermediate Grade in Baltimore

Materials
1. Dull gold burlap for background; flat pictures; black yarn; construction paper; corrugated paper

Methods
1. The bulletin was covered with burlap, and the pictures mounted on yellow khaki paper. The yarn was used to add design interest, and to help unify the arrangement
2. The map mount was given a 3-D effect by folding and scoring, then lacing with yarn

Children's participation
1. Helped assemble materials and put up

Sussman-Ochs Photo

A COLLECTION OF TALES!

A classroom bulletin board for Intermediate Grade

Materials
1. Yellow corrugated paper
2. Construction paper
3. Felt and metallic paper
4. Book jackets of four Newbery Medal winners

Method
1. The yellow corrugated paper was applied over white painted board The felt leaves were red, orange, brown, yellow and gold (metallic)
2. The fence and free shapes were cut from khaki-colored paper. The cats were orange, yellow and a deep maroon, outlined in contrasting ink
3. The skyline was cut to give a silhouette of rooftops

Children's Participation
1. They chose the jackets
2. Cut the leaves
3. Cut the "fence"
4. Helped to put up the material

Sussman-Ochs Photo

ENTIRE ZOO

Showing how 7th Graders in the Baltimore County Public Schools combined the various units for their papier-mache bulletin board project

THE ARTS:
A UNIVERSAL LANGUAGE

Done by 10th Grade students, Baltimore County Public Schools

COLONIAL PUNISHMENTS

Done by 11th Grade students, Baltimore County Public Schools

VEGETABLE PRINTING

Bulletin board arranged for an Intermediate Grade in Baltimore

Materials
    1. Children's vegetable prints
    2. White corrugated paper
    3. Wallpaper
    4. Construction paper

Methods and Colors
    1. The long prints were mounted by folding and scoring paper for a 3-D effect
    2. The short rectangles were mounted in frames made by scoring, folding and pinching corners
    3. Colors were black, white and silver

Children's Participation
    1. Executed the prints and helped arrange the display

Sussman-Ochs Photo

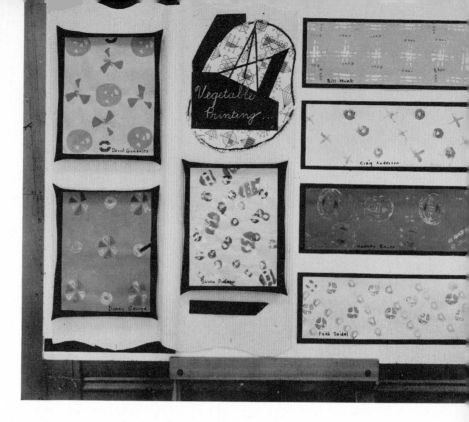

SHARING BOOKS

A classroom bulletin board for Intermediate Students

Materials
    1. Papier-mache book for centerpiece
    2. Black yarn and artificial leaves
    3. Miniature examples of types of book projects, e.g., diorama
    4. Play pencil (large)
    5. Construction and corrugated papers

Methods and Colors
    1. Title of board made from yarn stapled in letter form
    2. Miniature examples arranged on mats, color scheme around values of yellow, orange and brown
    3. The book centerpiece was made by applying papier-mache strips over a department store box and then painting with poster paint

Children's Participation
    1. Helped assemble materials and decide on what examples should be used
    2. Assisted with papier-mache project
    3. Helped put up

Sussman-Ochs Photo

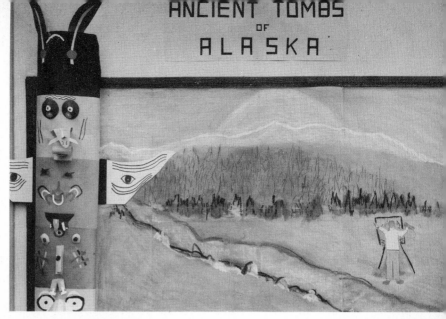

ANCIENT TOMBS OF ALASKA

5th Grade children's work, with totem pole in paper sculpture

Sussman-Ochs Photo

7TH GRADE PROJECT

With designs embroidered and appliqued in felt by students of the Baltimore County Public Schools

PAPER-SCULPTURED ANIMALS

For 9th Grade bulletin board, Baltimore County Public Schools
Cut designs for animal at left applied with soap eraser

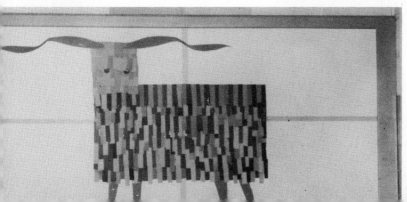

PAPER-SCULPTURED ANIMALS

For 9th Grade bulletin board, Baltimore County Public Schools
Texture applied to cutout animal by paper strips

SAFETY

Materials

Cardboard, traffic policeman's hat, belt and gloves, construction paper, old magazine safety pictures brought to class by children

Method

1. Since the heating pipes were in the way, blocking full view of the bulletin board, they were taken into account for the design, serving as support for figure of traffic officer, cut from cardboard

2. Shape of girl in foreground was obtained by having a large child stand against sheet of cardboard, and drawing around her

3. Two extra arms cut for policeman

4. Officer's cap, belt and gloves borrowed from former traffic headquarters of Baltimore's Police Commissioner, Bernard J. Schmidt

NOTE: At right may be seen a bulletin board devoted to "Best Books for Fifth Grade," with simulated book and prize ribbons

Sussman-Ochs Photo

GEOMETRIC SHAPES

This long bulletin board area above classroom blackboard displays a permanent exhibit featuring geometric shapes drawn and prepared by the children. Items were cut from vivid shades of construction paper and outlined with black

Sussman-Ochs Photo

PAPER-SCULPTURED ANIMALS

For 9th Grade bulletin board, Baltimore County Public Schools
* Eraser-cut design on animal's body
Curled paper on mane and tail

Art gum cut out, dipped in paint, then impressed on the paper

PER-SCULPTURED BIRDS

For 9th Grade bulletin board, Baltimore County Public Schools
Texture applied by curled paper, pasted on paper bodies

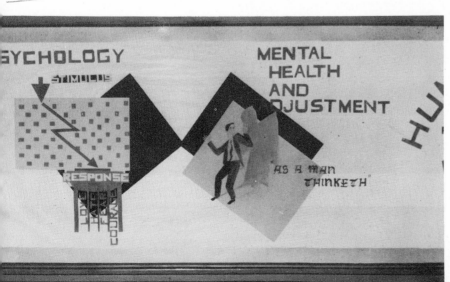

PSYCHOLOGY

Done by 12th Grade students, Baltimore County Public Schools

HOW PLANTS GROW

Materials and Colors
    Construction paper, tissue paper, co
    ored plastic, seeds, paint, ink
    Greens, blue and black, on white

Method
    1. Bulletin board as backdrop o
       garden corner in classroom
    2. Real seeds attached to cardboar
       with glue
    3. Paper plants show how a see
       grows and grows and grows
       (Children can help cut leaves fror
       both construction paper and tissu
       paper)

Sussman-Ochs Phot

"BREAKING UP" LARGE BULLETIN BOARD AREA

7th Grade, Baltimore County Public Schools
    At left—Embroidered designs
    At right—Original Christmas card designs
    Dividing the sections are multi-colored cutout paper circles attached to strip with center staples, to suggest Christmas decorations

RELIGION: MAN'S SEARCH FOR GOD

Done by 10th Grade students, Baltimore County High School

MAN'S SEARCH FOR GOD

Done by other 10th Grade Students, Baltimore County Public Schools

OUR COUNTRY'S FOUNDATIONS

Done by 11th Grade students, Baltimore County Public Schools

AMERICAN HISTORY CORE
(Correlated Subjects)

7th Grade, Baltimore County Public Schools

Classroom bulletin board divided into five panels:

Central general theme, other four representing significant events in American history

All cutout paper decorations

Simplicity stressed; paper waves to simulate water; prow of ship shown to represent person on deck

OUR FOREFATHERS DEFEND THEIR RIGHTS AS FREE MEN

7th Grade CORE (Correlated subjects) bulletin board, American history, Baltimore County Public Schools

Eagle wings extended to form background on which to place other cutout items, all paper

Black backdrop

(PAGES IN) THE STRUGGLE FOR FREEDOM

7th Grade CORE (Correlated subjects), American history, Baltimore County Public Schools

All decorations done with paper sculpture

Note design carried above bulletin board

PEOPLES OF THE RIVER VALLEYS

Done by 10th Grade students, Baltimore County Public Schools

WORLD HISTORY AND PROBLEMS — ARTS

Done by 10th Grade students, Baltimore County Public Schools

ANIMALS AT ZOO, CLOSE-UP

Part of papier-mache project for 7th Grade students, Baltimore County Public Schools
    Giraffe—Painting and yarn
    Llama—Painted white, then covered with looped white yarn
    Skunk—Painted
    Cage made in school shop

BASIC DRIVES

Done by 12th Grade students, Baltimore County Public Schools

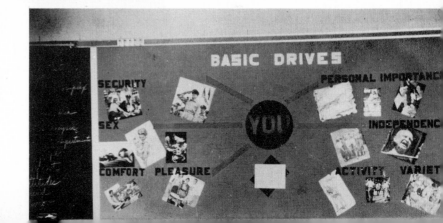

CAN YOU MAKE WENDY, THE HAND-PUPPET?

Materials and Colors

    Tag board, cardboard, fabric, tape, spool of thread, scissors, raw cotton, pin-cushion, buttons, miniature parasol, butterfly pin, yarn, paper doilies

    Red, white, yellow, pink, orange, purple, olive green

Method

  1. Outline own hand for shape cut from tag board

  2. Place each section of display on separate boards, then unify with cardboard strips

  3. Arrangement

    a. Fabric folded and taped on back of board

    b. Real articles and cutouts showing makings of puppet attached

    c. Letters may be cut from paper

    d. Sheer fabric used to show hand under puppet, but any fabric can serve in the actual preparation.

On this display a teacher could cut things out and with a pencil lightly indicate where each item is placed. As she is teaching the subject each piece may be applied to board with pin and hammer. When lesson is over the display is complete and can stay up as a decorative display

Sussman-Ochs Photo

WE HAVE GOOD HABITS

Materials and Colors

Fabric, construction paper, wallpaper, cloth adhesive tape

Brown, blue, green, yellow, tan, on white (most of the colors echoing tones in wallpaper design)

Method

1. In a school where there is little or no display space, find an area such as this door of a supply closet in hall—for display on a general topic, or rule to be remembered—through words (for older children) or pictures (for younger children)

2. Fabric used for clothing duplicated that in children's uniforms worn in this school, which the youngsters identified with themselves

3. Facial expressions on all children different, even though same paper shapes were cut

4. Black cloth adhesive tape holds parts of poster together and at the same time separates areas

5. Poster may be taken down in parts and used separately when display is over

Fred Worthington Photo

THE FAMILY

Materials and Colors

Strip of colored paper, ink

Red, orange, tan, black, yellow, pink, on white

Method

1. Strips picked from paper scraps in a print shop were used for house and cutouts decorating this elementary school bulletin board

Fred Worthington Photo

CONFUCIUS

Done by 10th Grade students, Baltimore
County Public Schools
   (Caption letters cut from paper)

ANIMALS AT ZOO, CLOSE-UP

For 7th Grade papier-mache bulletin board
project, Baltimore County Public Schools
   Ostrich—Trimmed with Easter grass
   Bear—Texture applied with papier-
   mache while shaping
   Zebra—Trimmed with yarn

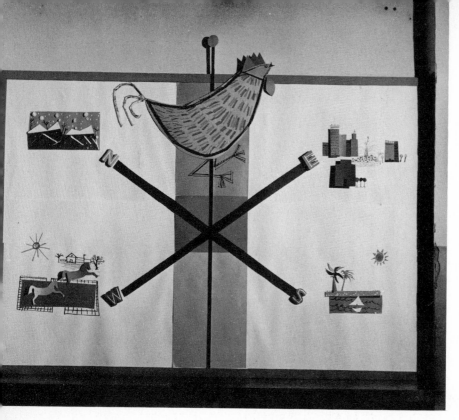

Note: Background paper used to cover dirty bulletin board later taken down and re-used in a torn-paper project

WEATHER VANE

Materials and Colors
> Construction paper, wood strip, pain[t], ink, cutout letters
> White, orange, yellow, red, purple, blue, black, on white paper

Method
1. Using materials available in school, this bulletin board design wa[s] created to show the importance o[f] white space in an art work
2. Simple shapes, with minimum o[f] cutting
3. Strip of wood down center for extra support, extending above display area
4. Construction paper pinned ou[t] from board to give 3-D effect

5. North } Created simply, to give small children a feeling of difference in areas of our country. Topic tied in with discussion on weather as well as geography. Also gave a decorative air to room throughout school year

East }

South }

West }

ANIMALS AT ZOO, CLOSE-UP

Papier-mache figures made by students for 7th Grade bulletin board, Baltimore County Public Schools
> Lion—Trimmed with paper curls
> Giraffe—Trimmed with yarn
> Camel—Trimmed with excelsior
> Cages made in school shop

CHAPTER SIX / "HOW-TO" HELPS

Some of the most beneficial display results can be achieved with simple materials and techniques. For example, an inexpensive insect spray gun will often serve the purpose of an expensive paint spray. Kitchen or stationery sponges cut to shape and painted, will make adequate "trees" and "shrubs," eliminating the purchase of costly commercial miniatures.

Here are some ideas and suggestions likely to add to the interest and effectiveness of posters and bulletin boards.

STENCILS—ESPECIALLY USEFUL FOR REPEAT PATTERNS

Spray—Keep stencil in place on board with pins. Pour paint into an insect spray gun, or blow with a fixative mouth spray for smaller areas, depending on the effect desired. (Wash out spray gun immediately after using, to prevent clogging)

Spatter—Rub a toothbrush or stiff bristle brush over a piece of screening held horizontally about six inches above the stencil

Dry Brush—Where direct application of paint is needed, for small areas such as tree leaves, brush out excess paint, then brush in from edges of a stencil

Tomato Cartons—Make good stencils

LETTERING—The above processes are excellent for caption variants with:

Cutouts—Letters cut from magazines or headlines of newspapers, and pasted together

Chalk Letters—Similar to those a child would print on a blackboard

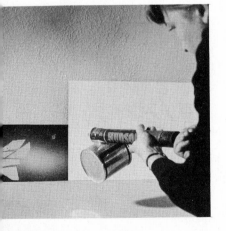

T SPRAY IN ACTION

Method

1. An insect gun and poster paint thinned out about "half and half" with water, is an easy way to get good results
2. The spray is here being used to illustrate the "blast" from a rocket. Also shown on the poster are cardboard shapes blocked with poster paint

Sussman-Ochs Photo

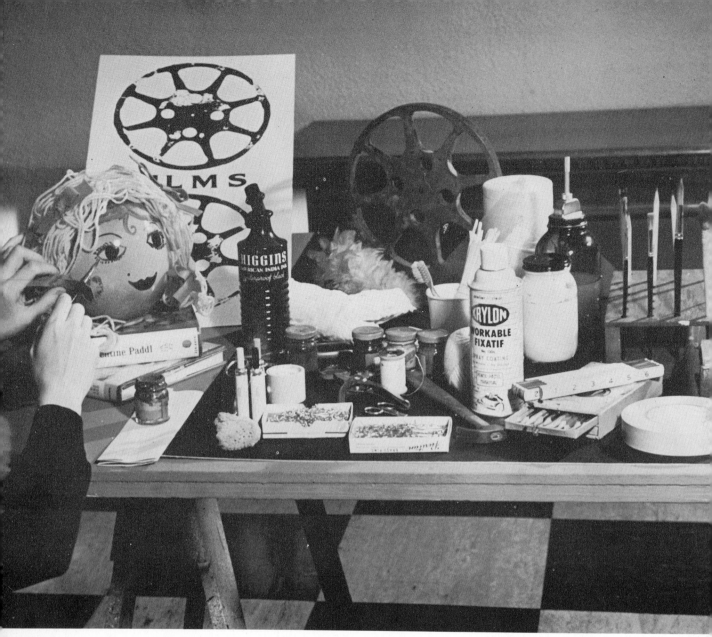

Sussman-Ochs Photo

WORKING TOOLS FOR POSTERS AND BULLETIN BOARDS
At left is a vase being transformed into a woman's head, for use with cookbooks and other homemaking volumes. Yarn used as hair. Back of the vase is a poster printed with the empty film reel seen at rear center

RDBOARD BLOCK PRINT
ROCESS (1)

Draw simple pattern for snowflake on round piece of tag board

Cut with mat knife

Paste design onto a circle of cardboard the same size or slightly larger

With a stipple brush, cover with white poster paint

ARDBOARD BLOCK PRINT
ROCESS (2)

Press pattern down on poster. The design will come up sharply or subtly, depending on amount of pressure applied

BLOCK PRINTS—Also suited to repetitive design

Battleship Linoleum—May be cemented on a wooden block and a **reverse** design can be cut into it with gouges. This process can be used when a large number of posters of the same design are needed. When the design is simple and only one color is called for, it can substitute for a silk-screen job

*Cardboard Prints—This is an easier and more primitive method of block printing, and can be used when only four or five display pieces are needed. The design is cut out of cardboard with scissors or linoleum knife. Poster paint is then applied to the surface with a felt wall roller. While still wet this is placed face down on another piece of cardboard, and pressure is applied. When it is raised the reproduction will be in evidence

*Old rubber from heavy innertubes may be treated in the same way, and small designs may be printed with cutout soap erasers

Felt Wall Paint Roller—Useful for the purposes mentioned above; also, for coating white poster board solidly without streaking if colored cardboard is not available

Potatoes—Can be cut out and used to make effective block prints on poster board, paper or cloth

Leaves—Can be painted and used as prints

COMBS—Drawn across wet paint can create unusual grass and water effects

STRAIGHT OR CURVED LINES—To produce thin lines, such as the stems of flowers or the pages of a book, apply paint of the color desired to the edge of cardboard strips, and press onto surface of poster or bulletin board

SPONGE—Useful in applying paint to backgrounds, for water effects, sky, a pebbly, sandy effect, trees, leaves

INK RESIST—This technique, combining paint and ink, can be used to attain an old woodcut effect. White paint is brushed on a fairly sturdy white paper surface where the white will appear on the finished design. After this has dried India Ink is flooded over the entire area. The paint acts as a **resist** and keeps the ink from penetrating the paper where the white portion of the design will appear. When dry, this is held under running water, which washes off the paint, and the completed art finish is visible. Color, if desired, may be applied by using colored inks on the white area

COLORED CONSTRUCTION PAPER — Suitable for covering large areas with color. Also, good for figures, especially in large areas, to show dimension, such as attaching a cutout arm onto the poster or bulletin board at the shoulder level—letting the arm protrude and then attaching it to the display piece at the hand. For feathers, leaves, animal tails, children's hair, construction paper can be cut and curled with scissors

CHILDREN'S BUILDING BLOCKS—Certain letters in relief— as A, I, H, O, T, V—make excellent block prints for lettering captions. (Be careful not to use letters that will appear in reverse)

MATERIALS TO CREATE DIMENSION

Paper Doilies—For snowflakes, lace collars and cuffs, petticoats, Valentine hearts, Christmas angels, flower bouquets

Buttons—For eyes on figurines, "wheels" for paper and cardboard vehicles, centers of flowers, parts of clothing

Twigs—Actual tree twigs painted or sprayed are very effective

Tissue Paper—Can be pleated and gathered for clothing on figures

Ice Cream Sticks—Can be glued and painted for decorative purposes

Wooden Dowels—Any number of uses—poles, flower stems, umbrellas, trees, etc.

INK RESIST

Method
1. Draw design on paper or b with wax crayons. If colored are used on paper, some o color will be retained
2. India ink is then flooded ove entire area and allowed to thoroughly
3. (see right) A razor blade (p ably a dull one) is held at a angle to the paper and scr over the design. Where the in been applied over the crayo surface will come off, but th waxed areas will remain virt unaffected. This technique i pecially good for achieving "antique" finish

Artist, Emily
Sussman-Ochs

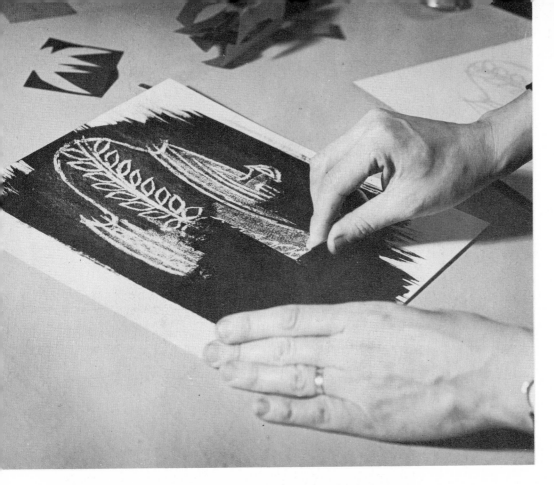

**INK RESISTS SHOWING
COMPLETED PRODUCTS**

Mailing Tubes—Especially handy on large displays—adaptable as arms and legs for figures, guns, etc.

Thread, Rope, Yarn, Embroidery Cotton or Silk—Hair, animal tails, swing "ropes"

Map Pins—Centers of miniature flowers, buttons on clothing, bracelets, earrings

Metallic Paper—Gold, Silver, especially useful for Christmas-type decorations

Raw Cotton and Steel Wool—Hair, animal fur, clouds, rabbits, piles of snow, and a variety of other things

Pipe Cleaners—Stems of flowers, trees, figures

Sandpaper—Both light and dark, fine or heavy-textured, can be cut into assorted shapes and used "as is" or painted. The same is true of corrugated paper or any other material that lends itself to gluing

Paper Boxes and Egg Cartons—Can be cut, painted and used for different designs

Artificial Flowers and Natural Materials—Leaves, seed pods, weeds, corn, sea shells, dried flowers, feathers, can be used as decoration, particularly in connection with the changing seasons

Paper Accordian-Pleated Fans—Can be inverted to form the lower part of a female figure. The upper part can either be cut from a picture in a discarded magazine, or made from pipe cleaner or twisted wire

Wire Coat Hangers—For making mobiles

Green Sawdust—The type used in Christmas gardens makes realistic "grass" when sprinkled on plastic glue, and sand handled in the same way makes a good "beach"

Coffee Grounds—Can represent earth

CARDBOARD PRINTING PROCESS (1)

Many interesting things can be done with cardboard edges. First of all, decide on length of lines involved in making design, then cut cardboard to these various sizes.

Have a pan of paint mixed to proper color and dip cardboard edge into the paint, then apply to board over lines previously drawn with pencil. In the photograph shown here the subject is to be a tree, so several lines must be printed to give necessary thickness to the trunk

Sussman-Ochs Photo

CARDBOARD PRINTING PROCESS (2)

A smaller piece of cardboard is used to print the branches, by impressing single lines. Should a rounded line be desired, use the same plan, but hold edge of cardboard to form curve

ADDITIONAL TIPS

Plastic Glue, with water and foreign material, such as aquarium gravel in colors or white, can be used with poster paint to create the illusion of 3-D buildings, roads, roofs, garden walks (other materials that can be combined with paint for the same purpose are sand, small stones, sawdust)

A Paint Base called Polyvinyl Acetate can be used as glue. This acts as a binder, so that the paint and foreign materials will hold together. Plastic-based glue can withstand extreme heat, a condition to be considered if a poster or bulletin board is near a sunny window

Fabrics can be dipped in undiluted showcard color or casein paint, and will dry very stiff

Pot Cleaners, obtainable in various colors, small aluminum discs used by roofers, air conditioner and furnace filters, can be converted into trees and mountains

Aluminum Plates of the type used in freezers, small pie plates, fluted cup cake containers in assorted colors, masking tape in different widths and colors, can be cut into diversified shapes and used on posters and bulletin boards

Chicken Wire, Thin Wire on Spools, Screening, Corks, Lace, Net, and a host of other items available in hardware stores, dime stores, stationery stores and others can add interest to display work in many ways

Bottles—Empty plastic detergent bottles suggesting figure shapes, may become girls or women for display purposes, by painting faces on the caps, adding hair made of yarn, and paper or fabric clothing.

PAPIER-MACHE "SCULPTURE"

Persons interested in papier-mache may fashion the basic armature by using cardboard tubes from wax paper, paper towels or bathroom tissue; also, from boxes of various sizes and shapes—the round cereal boxes, the square or rectangular cracker, cookie, stationery or other boxes.

For instance, a cardboard tube remaining from a roll of wax paper will make an excellent "neck" for a giraffe, while discarded bathroom tissue tubes can represent the "legs." Box construction is particularly applicable for "buildings," but on occasion may be adapted to animal figures.

A twisted coat hanger with a roll of newsprint around it can also serve satisfactorily as an armature. High school students may prefer to work with hard wire or wire mesh bent into the desired shapes. For youngsters in the intermediate grades tube or box construction, or flexible wire, is usually easier to handle.

PAPIER-MACHE PROCESS

1. Mix wheat paste with water until thick and very smooth. Store in covered container 24 to 36 hours.

2. Tear old newspapers into strips about ¾" wide. One by one, saturate half the quantity with the paste. As each wet strip is applied to the armature, cover with a dry strip. Continue this until the form has been sculptured into the desired shape. (Use crumpled facial or bathroom tissue to model the smaller heads, features, hands, and other areas where detail is important. For clothing and other "soft" representations, tissue paper may be used as the final covering).

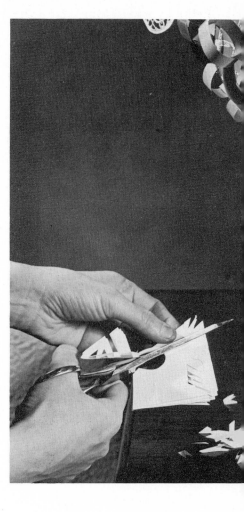

CUTTING "SNOWFLAKE"

Method
1. Cut square of lightweight pa[per] or metallic wrapping paper
2. Fold in half, then in half aga[in] to form smaller square
3. Next fold diagonally, as in old-fashioned diaper
4. Cut open design at each cen[ter] point, then work from corn[er] to cut a section of the sno[w] flake (See finished product [in] OLD-TIME CHRISTMAS TR[EE] The same type of decorati[on] may be used to advantage [on] posters and bulletin boards)

Sussman-Ochs Ph[oto]

OLD-TIME CHRISTMAS TREE

This tree has an old-world charm, and is very inexpensive to produce
Method

1. Ornaments cut from cardboard to represent pears, horns, cookies
2. "Cookies" decorated with thick white poster paint, for icing, some sprinkled
   with glitter in colors, to simulate colored crystallized sugar
   Small colored paper circles pasted on "cookies," to look like gum drops
3. Paper chain made from narrow, gaily-colored strips, formed into "links"
4. Artificial apples tied on with bits of ribbon
5. Rolled cardboard "candle," with bottom cut into fringe and bent, put on top,
   circle of color and "flame" added
6. Some snowflakes cut from doilies, others cut from paper as indicated in
   preceding picture

Sussman-Ochs Photo

PAPER FLOWER PROCESS (1)

Cut several sheets of construction paper the same size
On the top one draw the desired shape of a flower, then cut all the papers, using the drawing as a pattern (Colors of the paper used here: tan, orange, golden yellow, dark red—fall shades)

Sussman-Ochs Photo

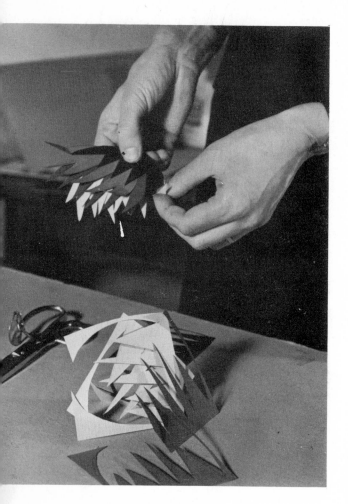

PAPER FLOWER PROCESS (2)

Fan out flowers, for most pleasing arrangement of colors and combinations
Cut a smaller flower shape in black paper, for contrast, and te overlapping papers

Sussman-Oc

PAPER FLOWER PROCESS (3)

Add a few extra petals, and paper stem

Sussman-Ochs Photo

PAPER FLOWER PROCESS (4)

Finished poster—black, white, blue, with flower done in colors already noted
Flower tones repeated in pans of water color

Method

1. Lettering done with "fat" brush flooded with paint (orange)
2. Paint box cut from black cardboard
3. "Glass" holding tools and flower cut from blue transparent plastic
4. Flower stem, paint brush, and pencil cut from construction paper
5. "Paints" are circles of construction paper. The white outlines around these discs, giving the illusion of paint pans, were done with paint on the bottom of a glass jar, printed as with the edge of cardboard

NOTE: The oversized box of paints and flower provide a decorative and striking effect for a large bulletin board

Sussman-Ochs Photo

JACK-IN-THE-BOX POSTER PROCES[

Draw light pencil lines on poster board,
ing placement of paper illustration
Cut hand, "head," eyes and mouth fro
struction paper
Fold long black paper in half, cut scep
sign, which has previously been dra
Open up . . . The design is the same
sides

JACK-IN-THE-BOX POSTER PROCES[

Paste pieces of brightly-colored tissue p
open work of sceptre, which now has a
look. From black paper cut out a
spring "

JACK-IN-THE-BOX POSTER PROCESS

Place "spring" on board. Now make collar out of gathered tissue paper pasted to a piece of black paper. The collar resembles a ruff

JACK-IN-THE-BOX POSTER PROCESS

Cut outline paper shapes for arms, and fill in with tissue paper pasted on the back. Paste down various pieces, and box, made of cardboard, lined with tissue. The spring is then added

JACK-IN-THE-BOX POSTER PROCESS

Branch display, The Enoch Pratt Free Library

Materials

      Cardboard, construction paper, tissue paper, gold discs, gold wire, paint, ink, pins

Method

      1. Various parts of figure jointed with gold discs
      2. Curl of gold wire for hair
      3. Tissue paper dots, arms, body, interior of box
      4. Black paper outline, sceptre, hand and spring
      5. Cardboard box, book title strips

NOTE: See progressive steps in preceding pictures

"CINDERELLA"

Library "Famous Books" Display
By 7th Graders, Baltimore County Public Schools
    Figures—Papier-mache
    Decorations—Cutout paper
    Apparel—Paper doilies on clothes

ENLARGING BY THE GRAPH METHOD

Small drawings from a variety of sources may be "blown up" for posters and bulletin boards, as illustrated, if no enlarging projector is available. Credit, of course, should be given to the original work.

As stated in "Effective Library Exhibits": "By dividing the original into small squares and duplicating the individual block lines in proportionately bigger squares, an exact enlargement is achieved."

CHAPTER SEVEN / THE CARE AND PRESERVATION OF DISPLAY MATERIALS

Posters and other bulletin board decorations which are to be kept for future use, require the most careful handling at all times. And the majority should be retained, if they have done their job well, for reasons of economy in time and money.

Cardboard and construction papers are lamentably susceptible to finger smudges and perspiration stains, while the items are in process, as well as during installation and dismantling. It must be borne in mind, too, that heavy pencil lines made with a sharp point are difficult to conceal or eradicate. Further, accidental paint spots can spoil an otherwise successful artistic effort.

Therefore, when a poster is in preparation, every precaution must be taken to guard against such mishaps. It is wise to work with a clean white cloth, to rest the hand that is inactive, thus avoiding unnecessary fingerprints.

Guide lines should be pencilled in lightly, for easy erasures. Good results in obliterating the pencil marks are usually obtained with a pink pearl or high quality art gum eraser. (For colored board a charcoal eraser is recommended). These reduce the danger of marks and smears.

If poster or casein paint drops fall unexpectedly outside the design area, a damp cloth lightly applied will sometimes remove the color without damage. Should this method fail, the thing to do is turn each spot into ornamentation, covering with attractive bits of colored paper, cardboard or fabric, or small related drawings, to supplement the main design.

When posters are mounted on bulletin boards by means of steel pins in the corners, extract the pins

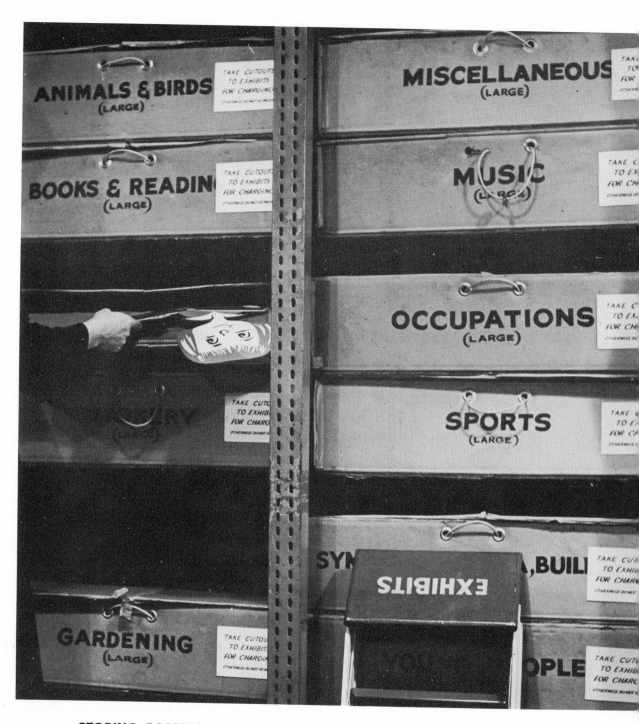

STORING POSTERS
Enoch Pratt Free Library

Large flat cartons suitably labeled and properly filed help maintain collection for re-use later on, thereby saving time, materials and money

Sussman-Ochs Photo

without bending, with long-nosed pliers, so that the pinholes will not become enlarged as the display is dismantled, and the pins, as well as the posters, may be used again.

If possible, store posters in enclosed, shelf-lined, dust-free areas, alphabetically by subject, for easy reference. Maintain a card file indicating title, size, colors and location for ready accessibility. Posters should lie flat, to prevent warping.

On occasions when three-dimensional treatments are involved, use separation boards or papers to keep other posters from weighing upon and crushing extending parts.

Should no shelf-lined, dust-free storage space be available, acquire some of the large, shallow corrugated paper cartons discarded by print shops. These are generally free for the asking, and will serve the purpose almost as well. The large, sturdy, waxed tomato cartons, with hinged lids, are also useful.

If greater depth is desired, oversize cartons may be requested from supermarkets, furniture or department stores, or purchased from paper box factories. These may be cut to the dimensions required, and the edges bound with masking or cloth adhesive tape for increased durability. Large cardboard and paper cutouts can be filed in similar containers.

For storing cutout letters, place strips of cardboard properly slit inside a carton, to form 30 compartments large enough to hold a given letter style. The carton should be deep enough to house the quantities of vowels and consonants likely to accumulate as the display program advances. Twenty-six of the compartments should be reserved for letters, the balance for numerals and punctuation symbols. A separate box is necessary for each cutout letter style in the display collection.

Filing cabinet drawers, cardboard boxes or large manila envelopes can take care of diverse three-dimensional objects used in displays. Whenever minor repairs are necessary after dismantling, these should be made before the pieces are put away. Properly labeled, the materials will be ready for instant use later on, as required.

Never mount or repair posters with plastic adhesive tape. This pulls the surface when detached, marring the appearance. Pins are recommended for mounting or, in the case of photographs or pictures which do not allow puncturing of corners, lay the items face down, place 10 or 12 thumb tacks or upholstery tacks (depending on thickness and weight of pictorial items) ½ inch from edge all around. Next affix a border of 1 inch masking tape all around, allowing the tack prongs to come through. The pictures then can be placed in proper position, by pushing the tacks into the bulletin board.

With reasonable care and handling display materials will last for a surprisingly long time, as they continue to prove their visual value to libraries and schools, supporting and enriching the printed and spoken word.

TOUCHING ON

THE SEASONS,
SOME HOLIDAYS
and
SPECIAL EVENTS

SUMMER

SUMMER

Materials and Colors
Felt or construction pap[er]
tissue paper, paint, c[ard]
board, cut-out letters
Brown, green, hot p[ink]
strawberry pink, orange,
orange, on white

Method
1. Fruit cut from felt or c[on]
struction paper
2. Books made from ca[rd]
board and paper
3. Clothes for figures m[ade]
from tissue paper
4. Paper circles for "r[ed]
cheeks"

Fred Worthington Ph[oto]

WINTER

Materials and Colors
Ink, paper doilies, angora,
tweed, paper cutout letters
White, dark blue, brown, on
pale blue (dark blue mostly,
to contrast with the white
snowflakes)

Method
1. To make tree limbs,
press painted strips of
cardboard on backdrop;
then, when dry, brush
on transparent ink as an
overlay
2. Cut doilies into snow-
flakes
3. Angora ear muffs
4. Tweed scarf and coat
5. Construction paper faces,
legs, hair

Fred Worthington Photo

WINTER

UTUMN

Materials and Colors
  Fabric, paper, chalk, cutout letters, cardboard
  Tans, orange, brown, olive green, on white

Method

1. Fabric for wearing apparel
2. Small slates made of black paper pasted on white cardboard
3. *Back to School* written in chalk
4. Leaves cut from "fall-colored" paper, but real autumn leaves may be collected and used

Fred Worthington Photo

SPRING

Materials and Colors
  Tissue paper, construction paper, paint, cutout letters
  Greens, light and dark pinks, on white

Method

1. Blossoms cut from white paper, then a coat of ink applied, causing the flower to curl (simulating a real blossom as it dries)
2. Thick blobs of paint form center of blossoms
3. Tissue paper leaves (if display remains only a short time, real green leaves may be used)

Fred Worthington Photo

MAKE YOUR SPRING READING GROW

Materials and Colors

Cardboard, construction paper, acetate, pins, felt-tip pen, adhesive tape

Pale green, yellow, yellow green, lavender, blue, black, white

Method

1. Watering can is rolled construction paper fastened underneath with adhesive tape, with spout and handle added
2. Circles of cardboard are put down with pins (after placement is planned and indicated lightly with pencil)
3. Stems added by drawing with felt-tip pen against ruler
4. Leaves glued at stem, leaving other ends free, for 3-D effect
5. Lines drawn on leaves with felt-tip pen
6. Books attached to circles (by method described under TRAINS poster)
7. When display is completed strips of acetate may be bunched at spout of watering can, and spread out over balance of exhibit, to simulate spring rain

Sussman-Ochs Photo

SPRING TIME IS READING TIME

Material and Colors

Tissue paper, construction paper, cardboard, poster paint

Blue, purple, green, on white

Method

1. Flower and leaves made of tissue paper
2. Construction paper pot
3. Lines of stem and book pages printed by using edge of cardboard strip, dipped into poster paint

Note: The happy, smiling flower, simplicity and abundant white space contribute to pleasant mood of the poster. The lettering style and placement suggest gaiety and lightness of tone

Fred Worthington Photo

SPRING SEED CATALOGS

Materials and Colors
Patterned paper, construction paper, cardboard, paint, ink
Yellows, red, orange, greens, blue-green, black, on white

Method
1. Smock cut from old magazine pages showing illustrations of printed fabrics
2. Books made of paper or cardboard, or real seed catalogs may be used

Fred Worthington Photo

SUMMER READING

Materials and Colors
Cardboard, construction paper, tissue paper
Black, orange, olive green, yellow, on white

Method
1. Turtle appears to be crawling, because it is pinned away from the backdrop, to give a 3-D effect
2. Grass blades made from tissue in olive green — a good contrast to the oranges and yellow of sun and turtle
3. Whole effect is simple, giving a feeling of summer leisure and reading enjoyment

Fred Worthington Photo

VACATION BOUND?

Materials and Colors

String, real hat, fabric scarf, flag, cardboard, construction paper

Dark green, light green, yellow orange, red, pink, on yellow

Method

1. Cut letters in style conveying a cheerful, carefree attitude, as identified with a vacation
2. Cut arms, legs and head separately, moving around on sunny yellow board until a pleasing movement-type appearance is achieved
3. Beach shoes are tied onto the feet with string
4. A real hat is used
5. The flag is poked into the crown just for fun, and to add a 3-D effect
6. If poster is large enough, a real book may be attached to hand

Fred Worthington Photo

GO PLACES WITH BOOKS

Materials and Colors

Cardboard, construction p a p e r, paint, ink

White, orange, yellow, gray, on black

Method

1. Figures cut from paper and pasted on slant, to show feeling of movement
2. Bus cut out of cardboard and pinned to give the appearance of depth

Fred Worthington Photo

SUMMER VACATION READING EXHIBIT
Los Angeles Public Library

"The illustration is paper sculpture, utilizing bright colored paper, adding dimension to an otherwise flat presentation."
Display by Anton H. Schedl

ANOTHER VACATION THEME
Los Angeles Public Library

"Effectively presenting the paper-sculptured mermaid figure as a focal point . . . Display artist uses a variety of paper, but finds that gift wrapping paper is always reliable. Paper is stapled and glued. With a little care it can be used more than once."
Exhibit by Anton H. Schedl

BOOKS FOR JUNE BRIDES

Materials and Colors

Dime store artificial flowers and veiling, to create bridal effect. Drawing of face, or magazine picture, or photo of fashion head in newspaper or fashion magazine may be used — the larger, the better

Pale blue-green, pink, purple

Method

1. Background is made by working with sponge wet with inks in above colors, rubbing across a slightly damp surface of board
2. Book cut from board treated in the same way, and scored in the middle after letters are applied. Pale bride colors are used on white for the book

Fred Worthington Photo

PICNIC TIME

Materials and Colors

Real plaid napkin, construction paper, cardboard, paint, ink

Red, black, white, purple, orange, green, tan, on white

Method

1. Figure of woman cut from two triangles of construction paper, with points pasted together for "waist"

Fred Worthington Photo

READING
(Branch display, Enoch Pratt Free Library)

Materials and Colors
Patterned wallpaper, cardboard, paint, construction paper
Fall colors, including pale to deep oranges, tans, yellows, dark rich reds and olive green, on white

Method
1. Paper cut to resemble opened book, with page lines done with cardboard edge dipped into paint, curved, and printed
2. Stems made with straight cardboard edges dipped in paint
3. Flowers made of paper — bits of patterned paper cut from linings of old envelopes, and saved over a considerable period — and fabric
4. Book binding made from patterned wallpaper
5. Letters follow the shape of book

Sussman-Ochs Photo

IT'S FALL AGAIN

Materials and Colors
Glove, twig, tissue paper, construction paper, dowel sticks, paint
Red, yellow, blue, white, black, greens, oranges

Method
1. Real glove for hand
2. Twig from a tree, with tissue paper leaves glued on
3. Buttons are ends of dowel sticks, painted lines represent buttonholes and stitching on sweater

Sussman-Ochs Photo

113

WINTER READING

Materials and Colors

Construction paper or felt, felt-tip pen, cardboard, ink

Black, tan, yellow, blue, orange, on white

Method

1. Cut books, hats and ear muffs from construction paper or felt
2. Felt-tip pen used for black lines

Fred Worthington Photo

FOLLOW THE SUN BY BOOK

Materials and Colors

Cardboard, green transparent plastic, textured, solid and patterned paper, paint

Reds, yellows, oranges, pinks, black, on white

Method

1. Hand-lettering
2. Book center of sun pinned away from background
3. Green transparent "lenses" in sun glasses
4. Sun's rays cut from cardboard, with textured, solid and patterned papers in sun colors pasted on

Fred Worthington Photo

EASTER

Materials and Colors

    Decorated egg shells, baby's breath, hat pin, construction paper, razor blade or mat knife, satin ribbon, ink

    Black, multi-colored decorated eggs, pink, purple, on white

Method

1. Eggs blown out, then decorated
2. Baby's breath painted white
3. Large hat pin to secure paper around bouquet
4. Construction paper book — one side flat, the other curved, to give 3-D depth
5. Lettering may be traced from a magazine, blown up (graph method), put on construction paper and cut out with razor blade or mat knife
6. Bird has a "dressed-up-in-Easter-best" look, because of simple cutout, high hat, and satin ribbon "bow tie"

(Same pattern used for cutting body of bird as used on rooster on weather vane bulletin board — Keep patterns and re-use whenever possible. This saves much work)

Fred Worthington Photo

LENTEN READING DISPLAY
The Free Library of Philadelphia

"A simple stand-up exhibit made for a table in the Education, Philosophy and Religion Department . . . Flat homosote was used for the background and encircled with a wooden frame. The colors were a light purple accented with white, green and black. The unit was placed so that it could be seen from the hall and attracted many visitors to browse."

FLAG DAY, JUNE 14

Materials and Colors
> Miniature American flags, construction paper, feathers, cutout letters
> Red, white, and blue, on navy blue

Method
1. Legs, guns, hats and faces for all figures, cut at the same time, group by group
2. Feathers cut from red feather duster and stuck in hats
3. Bodies formed by large letters and numerals pinned away from back
4. Real American flags pinned, with balance of parade, to bulletin board

Sussman-Ochs Photo

HALLOWEEN

Materials and Colors
> Nylon stocking, pipe cleaners, cloth tape, paint, cutout letters
> Royal blue, black, gold, yellow

Method
1. Cobweb made of discarded nylon stocking (this one had some gold nylon threads) pulled and pulled until it was all ripped, then pulled again at various places and attached with pins
2. Spider legs made of painted pipe cleaners, body and head of cloth tape
3. Moon printed with a round piece of cardboard painted yellow
4. Eerie plant effect achieved by putting black ink on the bottom of the poster and blowing it upward
5. Cutout letters, appropriate to the mood of the poster, pasted on

Sussman-Ochs Photo

HALLOWEEN

Materials
> White construction or typing paper, transparent adhesive tape, felt-tip pen, ink

Method
1. "Scary" little ghosts made of white paper, with small wedges trimmed off top ends
2. Crumpled at neck, fastened with adhesive tape underneath each figure
3. Faces drawn with felt-tip pen

Sussman-Ochs Photo

THANKSGIVING

Close-up of apple being pinned to poster

Sussman-Ochs Photo

THANKSGIVING

Prepared by Frank Cipolloni

Materials and Colors

Cover paper, tissue paper, cardboard, cellophane paper, ribbon, artificial fruit, pins, pliers

Black, pink, deep rose, lavender, green, aqua, on white

Method

1. Cornucopia made of black paper
2. Assorted tissue and cellophane paper superimposed on wallboard and pinned to backdrop, to give dimension
3. Ribbons, apples, grapes added, pinning through wire stems, and bending pins like Christmas ball hangers

Sussman-Ochs Photo

CHRISTMAS GREETINGS

Materials and Colors
Cotton balls, evergreen twigs, satin ribbon, velvet ribbon and fabric, cardboard, construction paper, legal seals, ink
Red, green, black, white
Method
1. Basket and balloon drawn with felt-tip pen
2. Santa Claus drawn on tracing paper and cut out of construction paper
3. Fabric pasted on costume area
4. Santa's leg in basket was drawn separately and painted to look like velvet of his suit, then cut out and attached to basket, with black "basket lines" drawn over leg to make it appear that leg was inside
5. Santa pinned down, beard (cotton balls) attached with glue
6. Cardboard "books", with paper "pages" pinned at center

Sussman-Ochs Photo

HOLIDAY BOOKS

Materials and Colors
Patterned paper in bright colors; construction paper, ink or paint
Black on white cardboard
Method
1. If poster is small, use fabric or gay wrapping paper cutout circle; if large, use wallpaper
2. Lines can be cut from paper, or drawn with ink or paint
3. If the poster is a large one, letters and lines could also be done in string and starch (see "Boating" illustration), and painted black (The only color is in the patterned paper. Choose a bright-colored pattern, strong in design)

Sussman-Ochs Photo

HAPPY HANUKAH

Materials and Colors

Construction paper, aluminum foil, glossy paper, cardboard, paint, pins, felt-tip pen, ink

Blue, purple, turquoise, silver, black, white, orange

Method

1. Candles and "Menorah" cut from large sheets of construction paper
2. Paper folded before "Menorah" is cut, so that both sides are identical. Center crease adds dimension to an otherwise flat poster
3. Candle holders cut from aluminum foil
4. Candle flames varying slightly in size — giving the illusion of flickering — cut from fire-bright shiny orange paper

Sussman-Ochs Photo

MERRY CHRISTMAS

Materials and Colors

Tissue paper, cardboard, metallic and red paint, pinking shears, white board

Red, gold, dark green, black, on white

Method

1. Tissue cut with pinking shears for seal-shape Christmas decoration (gold, black, red; paint used for tree and Santa)
2. Dark green books
3. Tree made by printing with edge of cardboard

Fred Worthington Photo

"CHRISTMAS WREATH" O
BOOK JACKETS
San Diego Public Library
(With Marianne Berlinde)

CHRISTMAS DISPLAY
Los Angeles Public Library

"Somewhat of a departure from the norm. The first floor wall cases are bedecked with certain animals of the forest in paper sculpture form. From time to time paper sculptures were animated by simple battery-operated motors. The Children's Department furnished an original verse (featured above the figure) to augment the children's books and the bear figure. Note the interesting use of canopy above the case."

Exhibit by Anton H. Schedl

WALL EXHIBIT
Los Angeles Public Library

"A brightly colored example of paper-sculptured figures . . . during the Christmas season. The element of simplicity was shown off to excellent advantage . . . Paper sculpturing is an excellent display medium, adding interest and animation to an exhibit with or without books"

Anton H. Schedl

CHRISTMAS BOOK FAIR EXHIBIT
Brooklyn Public Library

CHRISTMAS BULLETIN BOARD

By 7th Grade students, Baltimore County
Public Schools

Cut-out paper letters mounted on individual paper sheets, and outlined
with black chalk

Minstrels in various amusing poses and
decorations done with paper and chalk

Straw and styrofoam designs hanging
from lights

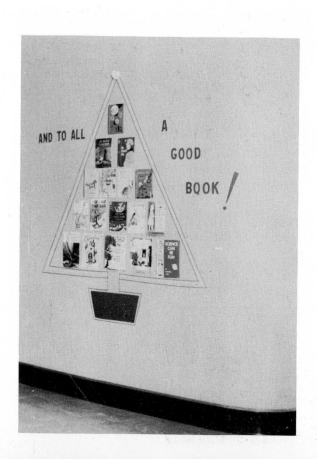

"CHRISTMAS TREE" OF
BOOK JACKETS
San Diego Public Library

FOR CHRISTMAS BULLETIN BOARD
(One Section)

By 7th Graders, Baltimore County Public Schools
  Bulletin board about 40' long, divided into 12 panels
  of gray, white and black, representing 12 days of
  Christmas, in cutout paper.
  Students worked on each sketch, after discussion
  with teacher, and best one was selected and cut out

CHRISTMAS BULLETIN BOARD
(One Section)

By 7th Graders, Baltimore County Public Schools
  Cutout paper figures
  Designs on clothes printed with soap eraser
  Design on background made with cardboard
  edges dipped in paint and sprayed gold

FOR CHRISTMAS BULLETIN BOARD
(Two Sections)
By 7th Graders, Baltimore County Public Schools

CHRISTMAS BULLETIN BOARD
(One Section)
By 7th Graders, Baltimore County Public
Schools

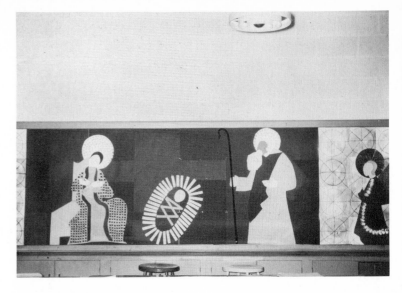

CHRISTMAS BULLETIN BOARD,
WITH SECTIONS JOINED
By 7th Graders, Baltimore County Public
Schools

CHRISTMAS BULLETIN BOARD
(One Section)
By 7th Graders, Baltimore County Public
Schools

CHRISTMAS BULLETIN BOARD (Panel-Type)
Work by 7th Graders, Baltimore County Public Schools

Placement by teacher, after discussion with
students

Panels divided by colored areas with circle or
star theme, mostly cutout paper

Stars made of styrofoam balls cut in half, with
straws inserted

Designs to represent wings are store-bought stars
pasted down

Theme adapted from early Italian angels playing
instruments

Angels in bright color

Colors in background—black, gray, white

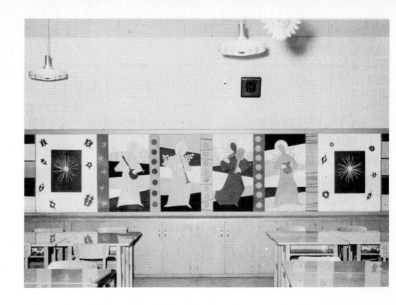

CHRISTMAS BULLETIN BOARD
(Sections Joined)
By 7th Graders, Baltimore County Public Schools

CHRISTMAS BULLETIN BOARD (One Section)
By 7th Graders, Baltimore County Public Schools

125

PART OF EXHIBITION OF STUDENTS' WORK
7th, 8th, 9th Graders, Baltimore County Public Schools

Papier-mache Animal—Painted and given texture
Background decoration:
　　Mosaics—Paper
　　Shapes in Space — Crayon rubbings and
　　"sketcho" (oil stick crayon)
　　Repeat Designs from Nature—Stencil
At right: Paper sculpture

PART OF EXHIBITION OF STUDENTS' WOR
7th, 8th, 9th Grades, Baltimore County Public Schoo
　　"Enlarged paper cutout taken from linoleum blo
　　print representing theme of exhibit"
　　Papier-mache Llama
　　Color experiments with crayon shapes

PART OF EXHIBITION OF STUDENTS' WORK
7th, 8th, 9th Grades, Baltimore County Public Schools

　　Close-up of:
　　　　Kachina Dolls—Pastels
　　　　Totem Poles—Paper Sculpture
　　　　Paper Masks, simulating animals—Paper Sculpture

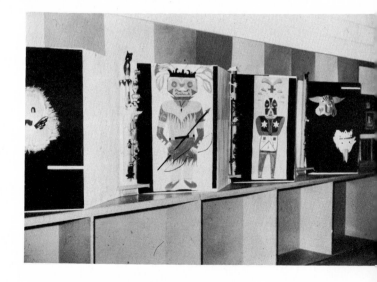

FOR CHRISTMAS BULLETIN BOARD (Panel-type)
By 7th Graders, Baltimore County Public Schools

Paper cage-line strips were extended to give dimensional effect

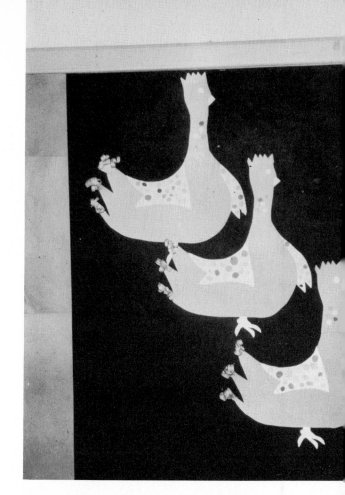

FOR CHRISTMAS BULLETIN BOARD
(Panel-type)
By 7th Graders, Baltimore County Public Schools
Curled cutout paper used for tails

FOR CHRISTMAS BULLETIN BOARD
(Panel-type)
By 7th Graders, Baltimore County Public Schools

Teachers and students discussed arrangement
Cut paper; metallic paper trim; paper doilies

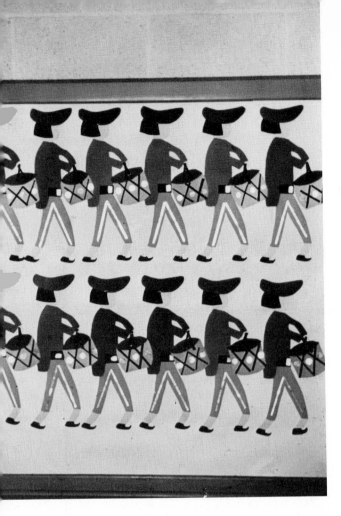

FOR CHRISTMAS BULLETIN BOARD (Panel-type)
By 7th Graders, Baltimore County Public Schools

All cut paper

FOR CHRISTMAS BULLETIN BOARD (Panel-type)
By 7th Graders, Baltimore County Public Schools

Cut paper; metallic paper trim

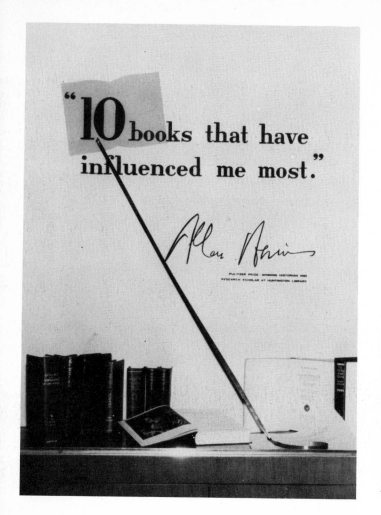

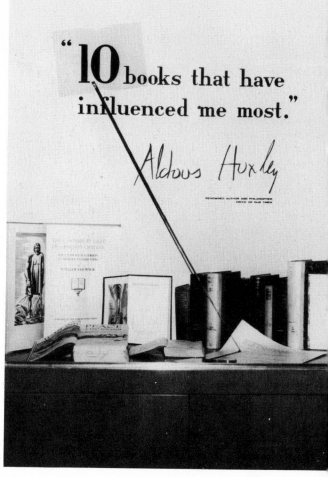

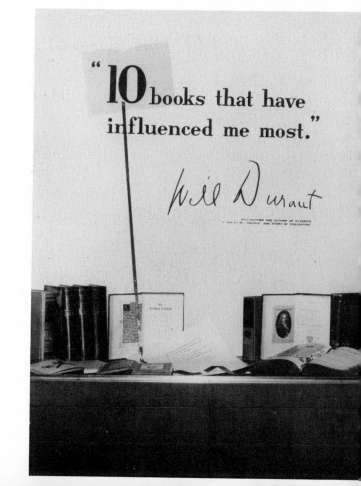

PART OF NATIONAL LIBRARY WEEK SERIES
Los Angeles Public Library

Promoting books recommended by famous personalities

PROGRESS REPORT, NATIONAL LIBRARY WEEK
Los Angeles Public Library

"An up-to-date Library building progress report was effectively displayed with photographs and maps . . . The above L shaped panel was devised to tell the public what the Los Angeles Public Library had been doing with the $6,400,000 bond issue money. The map at left explained in detail every branch building project progress to date, while the panel at right graphically depicted the old and the new with some human interest shots added"

Exhibit by Anton H. Schedl

PROGRESS REPORT, NATIONAL LIBRARY WEEK
Los Angeles Public Library

"The reverse side of the L shaped panel featured (at left) architect's drawings of buildings in process of construction or on the drawing boards. The panel at right is a giant photo blow-up of Johnny, who symbolizes all the youngsters who have recently been using Los Angeles Public Library services as they never have before"

Exhibit by Anton H. Schedl

UNITED NATIONS DISPLAY
Denver Public Library

Peg board covered with light [blue?]
paper background, decorated [with]
colored rectangles of paper and fl[ags]
of member nations

Exhibit by Janice White
Photo by Bob Gordon

STRICTLY FOR SECRETARIES

Materials and Colors
   Picture of typewriter, construction paper, cardboard, paint,
   ink
   White, black, blue, green, tan
   cardboard
Method
   1. By the graph method, blow
      up picture of typewriter
      found in a discarded maga-
      zine, and use its shape as
      a pattern for machine made
      from black construction
      paper
   2. Gray rounded lines painted
      on tan cardboard simulate
      wood grain

Fred Worthington Photo

CRUITING EXHIBIT,
TIONAL LIBRARY WEEK
Angeles Public Library

"The photographs told the story of the many and varied activities of a branch librarian and a children's librarian. The display included the following statement: 'What it takes to be a public librarian: A love of books . . . an enjoyment of people . . . and the knowledge of how to bring the two together. Challenging? Yes, and a profession worth considering now' "

Exhibit by Anton H. Schedl
Photo by Bert N. Snow

REFERENCE EXHIBIT,
NATIONAL LIBRARY WEEK
The Brooklyn Public Library

Questions and answers appear on the white blocks

BALTIMORE TEEN-AGERS PICK THEIR "TOP TEN"

A colorful bulletin board arranged by the Young Adult Division, Enoch Pratt Free Library, after a poll of young people's book favorites taken in connection with National Library Week.

Sussman-Ochs Photo

AMERICAN EDUCATION WEEK DISPLAY

With copies of the official poster mounted on contrasting cardboard, and related books and pamphlets placed on cardboard circles of harmonizing color. A center band of dark paint on the light cutout caption letters gives a two-toned effect.

Sussman-Ochs Photo

A MISCELLANY OF DISPLAY IDEAS

WORLD COOKERY

Materials and Colors

Bent wire, tinsel; painted, artificial or construction paper fruits (or pictures of *fruits and vegetables cut from discarded magazines), **real or cardboard** cook books

Turquoise, purple, greens, black, on white

Method

1. Clear acetate used for fruit bowl
2. Shape and decorate bent wire, topped by "candles"
3. Bird and cardboard books covered by tissue paper

* Type of fruits and vegetables used determine mood of poster. For everyday, simple cook books—apples, oranges, carrots, etc.; for more elegant type cook books, artichokes, pineapple, grapes, large strawberries

Fred Worthington Photo

DISHES FAVORING FISHES

Materials and Colors

Construction paper, cardboard, paint, ink

Pale green, black, dark red, pinks, oranges

Method

1. Background in four different reds, made of uncut sheets of construction paper
2. Finished poster is scored down center, forming "pages" of cardboard "book" it is attached to

Fred Worthington Photo

THE BATTLE OF THE BULGE, BOOKS FOR CALORIE COUNTERS

Materials and Colors
 Construction paper, cardboard, paint, ink, pictures of earrings and other items
 Turkey red, red, pink, purple, black

Method
1. Bow on hat, earrings, buttons, fruit, cake—all cut from pictures in discarded magazines

Fred Worthington Photo

GOOD GROOMING

Materials and Colors
 Wool yarn, satin ribbon, construction paper, cardboard, paint, string
 Orange, light purple, black, on white

Method
1. Braided wool for hair
2. Ribbon for bows
3. Small charms of cardboard on the string "bracelet"

Fred Worthington Photo

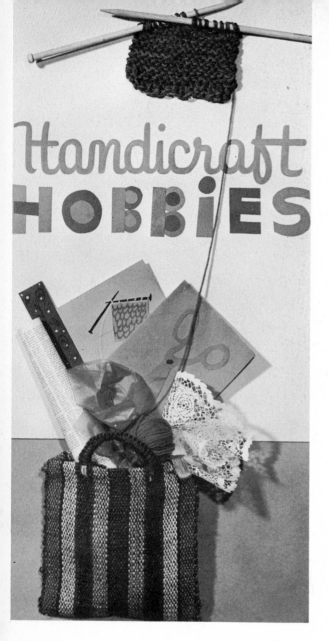

HANDICRAFT HOBBIES

Materials and Colors

    Wooden knitting needles, magazines, straw shopping bag, doily, wool, tissue paper, paint, construction paper, cutout letters

    Blue, tan, orange, black, white, gray

Method

1. Cutout letters pasted down for caption
2. Scarf end knitted in advance and pinned on
3. Shopping bag with books, doily to represent a hand-made handkerchief, ball of knitting wool, attached
4. Poster background in two tones—white on top and gray on bottom. Since poster had to be pieced, it looked better to use two colors, rather than one, with seam in evidence

Sussman-Ochs Photo

NEW ARRIVALS

Materials and Colors

    Wallpaper, ink, paint, construction paper, cardboard

    Blue-purple, light pink with purple tone, deeper pink, black, on white

Method

1. Wallpaper umbrella, with fringe painted on
2. Book lines printed with edge of cardboard dipped in paint

Fred Worthington Photo

PANEL-TYPE EXHIBIT
The Public Library of Cincinnati and
Hamilton County

**FREE-STANDING PANEL
EXHIBIT**
The Public Library of Cincinnati and
Hamilton County

RECESSED EXHIBIT
The Free Library of Philadelphia

"This simple figure was executed in ink on white no-seam paper. The hair was made from black construction paper and left unpinned at the edges so that it would appear dimensional. The kimono was borrowed from a Library patron and was pinned to give the effect of a woman in motion. The letters were cut from construction paper"

DISPLAY MOUNTED ON PEG BOARD
The Denver Public Library

Blue background, gray flannel sheep
Exhibit by Janice White
Photo by Bob Schott

FOR LARGE AND SMALL

Materials and Colors
Cardboard, crayon, construction paper
Green, purple, blue, black, white

Method

1. The large figure was done, and the small one copied, cut out, and pasted down next to the large one. (This could have been reversed, with the small figure drawn first, and the other enlarged by the graph method. In this case both would be exactly alike. They are not identical now)
2. Figures covered with ink, almost to outer line
3. Cardboard book cut at angle, joined at spine with black tape and bent, then pinned on with wallboard, to give 3-D effect. Finishing touches—hats, bows, faces—done with pen and ink.

Fred Worthington Photo

SALTY YARNS OF THE SEA

Materials and Colors
Cardboard, construction paper, dried fern (may be taken off the poster and used again), sequin material, paint

Method

1. Fern to simulate seaweed
2. Mermaid's lower body made of sequin material with the sequins punched out. The holes were painted in different colors.

Fred Worthington Photo

INTERIORS
Display arranged by Fine Arts Department
The Enoch Pratt Free Library

Materials and Colors
Book jackets, construction paper, crayon, cutout letters, book lists on home decoration
Tan, brown, green (these tones repeated in the book jackets, along with pinks, golds and reds)
Method
1. Floor plan from blueprint idea, used to set off jackets
2. Pocket holding book lists made of construction paper
3. Heavy division lines of construction paper, thin lines drawn with crayon
4. Paper backdrop too small to cover entire board, so panel of darker color was added, improving the design

Sussman-Ochs Photo

AFRICAN ART EXHIBIT
Los Angeles Public Library

"Original African art objects were borrowed from a local museum, enhancing the book titles displayed"
Exhibit by Bernice Barth, Hollywood Regional Branch

BULLETIN BOARD-TYPE EXHIBIT
Glendale Public Library

"With records, book jackets, newspaper clips, film reel applied. Color was rolled on with paint roller, or sponged. Letters were paper cutouts"

Display artist, Eloise M. Frain

"SPACE" EXHIBIT
Glendale Public Library

Using "enlarged book in full relief (a cardboard dummy from publishing house)"

Display artist, Eloise M. Frain

SEWING EXHIBIT
Glendale Public Library
"Colored paper, wallpaper, cotton yarn . . . hand-lettered script"

Display artist, Eloise M. Frain

HUMOR EXHIBIT
Glendale Public Library

"Cutout paper and wallpaper, cotton yarn 'strings', cutout paper F and H, script hand-lettered"

Display artist, Eloise M. Frain

READ THE DO-IT-YOURSELF BOOKS

Materials and Colors
> Book jackets, construction paper, cord, dowel stick, bank pins, paint, cardboard
> Black, bright blue, bright pink, orange, purple, on white

Method
> 1. The hat, being made right on the woman's head, includes: book jackets, paper shapes of spool of thread (with cord as thread), scissors and pin cushion, plus decorative features, such as flowers and grapes
> 2. Earrings are slices of a dowel stick
> 3. Real bank pins are stuck into pin cushion and mouth
> 4. Hand and needle cut from cardboard

Fred Worthington Photo

HELPS FOR HOMEMAKERS

Materials and Colors
> Velvet, string, cloth, cardboard, construction paper
> Various shades of blue, black, green, turquoise, yellow, green and tan

Method
> 1. Bits of velvet, string and end of fabric were used to make this poster

Fred Worthington Photo

144

BOOKS THAT BOYS LIKE

Materials and Colors
    Paper, string, yarn, crayon, cutout letters
    White, yellow, black, red, green
Method
    *1. Torn paper used for sun, boy's hair, grass sweater
    2. String used for pail handle
    3. Tie and flowers made from yarn
    * Torn paper was from paper which had previously lined a bulletin board, and was saved for future use when display was dismantled

Fred Worthington Photo

INDOOR GARDENING

Materials and Colors
    Tissue paper, cardboard, construction paper, paint, ink
    Blue, black, green, yellow, light red, on white
Methods
    1. Plants pinned away from the "window," with lettering on face of "sill"
    2. Tissue used as "fabric" for curtain
    3. Cardboard "shutter," cut at an exaggerated angle, pinned with a wedge of wallboard behind it

Fred Worthington Photo

INDOOR GARDENING

"BOOKS ARE MORE FUN THAN A BARREL OF MONKEYS"
as presented by the Talbot County Library, Easton, Md.

LIFE'S LIGHTER SIDE

Materials and Colors
    Tissue paper, rubber cement, paint, veiling, feather, ink
    Purple, greens, blue, black, on white

Method
1. Figures drawn, man smaller than woman, to add a touch of humor
2. Tissue paper cut same shape as figures and applied with rubber cement
3. Thick black line around major areas
4. Lettering placed to appear as if balanced on books

Fred Worthington Photo

LIFE'S LIGHTER SIDE

Materials and Colors
    Construction paper, crayon, paint, cutout letters, small pins, cardboard, wooden strip, ink
    Pinks, oranges, black, on white

Method
1. Shapes are pieces of construction paper, some cut, others right from the package
2. Books pinned away from board
3. Girl's hair and features drawn with crayon
4. Thin wooden strip used as temporary guide line for caption letters, which are pinned on
5. Pinheads touched up with sharp tip of paint brush handle and matching paints

Note: The humorous mood of this poster is evident throughout—in the face, shoes, shoe laces and figure placement

Fred Worthington Photo

POETRY EXHIBIT
The Toledo Public Library

"One of a series of poetry displays on 22" x 30" pedestal stand near Literature Division

FOR FICTION EXHIBIT
The Toledo Public Library

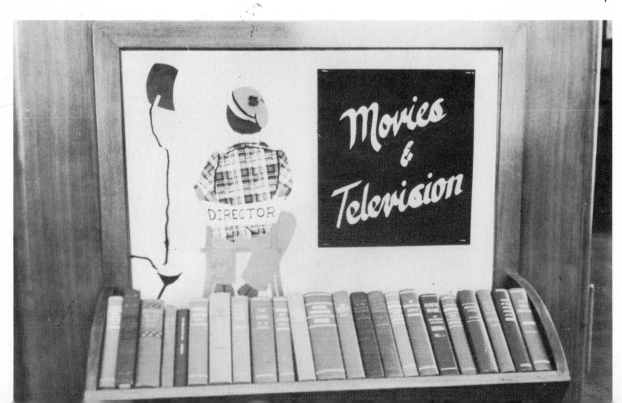

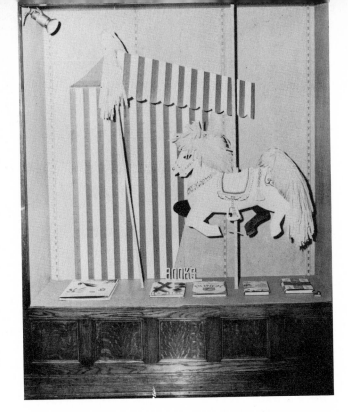

A SERIES OF EXHIBITS
The Long Beach Public Library

Depicting diversified Library services

Displays by John Lynch

RECESSED EXHIBIT
The Newark Public Library

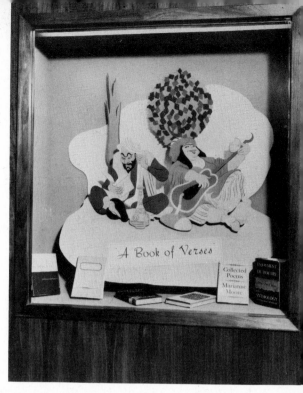

BILLBOARD-TYPE EXHIBIT
The Newark Public Library

(Idea adaptable for a bulletin board)
"This board, about 7 feet long and 4 feet high, was designed and painted by the exhibit artist (Miss Miller). The figures were two-dimensional, color especially pleasing. Used in a bank window."

"TALL TALE HEROES OF AMERICAN LEGEND"
The Newark Public Library

CLOCK-TYPE EXHIBIT
The Newark Public Library

"Make Time Worth While—READ"

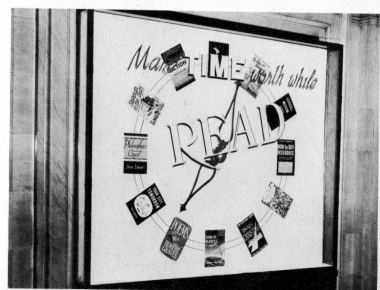

TER FOR PHILATELIC EXHIBIT
Minneapolis Public Library

Jsing "muted shades of pink, violet and green wallpaper
on white poster board"

POSTER FOR EXHIBITION ROOM
The Minneapolis Public Library

"Red, gray, black and white construction paper against
poster board"

Betty Beedle, artist

POSTER ANNOUNCING EXHIBIT
The Minneapolis Public Library

"Shades of green and aqua, black and white
wallpaper were used against a black poster board
background"

"DR. SEUSS" REPRESENTATIONS
IN THE CHILDREN'S ROOM
The Annapolis and Anne Arundel County Public
Library

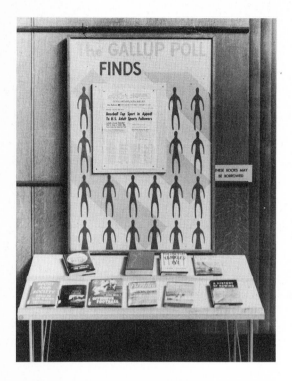

EXHIBIT FOR SPORTS FANS
The Brooklyn Public Library

"WINNIE - THE - POOH" DISPLAY
The Denver Public Library

Featuring the Pooh figures, real tree trunk,
and painted background

Photo by Bob Gordon

BOOK SECTIONS CONVERTED
TO DISPLAY AREAS
The Chicago Public Library

"A room exhibit in a store branch"

"KING ARTHUR" —
Library "Famous Books" Display
By 7th Graders, Baltimore County Public Schools

Figures—Papier-mache
Armor, Clothing—Aluminum foil, paper doilies
Hair—Raw cotton
Soap eraser designs on background

"IVANHOE" —
Library "Famous Books" Display
By 7th Graders, Baltimore County Public Schools

Figures of knights in foreground—Tongue depressors and cut paper
Pennants—Toothpicks and cut paper
Figures of knights on horseback—Cut by student with jigsaw, and mounted and painted at home
All designs printed with soap eraser (art gum cut out, dipped in paint, and impressed on the paper)

"PETER PAN" —
Library of "Famous Books" Display
By 7th Graders, Baltimore County Public Schools

Background bent for dimensional effect
Figures—Papier-mache
Clouds—Raw cotton

"TREASURE ISLAND" —
Library "Famous Books" Display
By 7th Graders, Baltimore County Public Schools

Figures—Papier-mache
Buildings—Cardboard boxes, covered and painted

153

POSTERS AT STACK ENDS
The Chicago Public Library

"Special displays at end of book stacks in branch building"

CHILDREN'S ART

Materials and Colors
    Crayon, book, ink
    Blue, orange, yellow, green, red, black,
    on white board
Method
1. Display for children's art and books about children's art, drawn in crayon as a child might do (it might be well to use a youngster's drawing)
2. Real book
3. Letters accurate, yet placed as a child might arrange—easy to read, even for a youngster

Fred Worthington Photo

STEP INTO STORYLAND

Materials and Colors
    Silver metallic paper, tissue paper, cardboard, ribbon, twisted wool yarn, construction paper, gold tassel, ink, paint
    Purple, light and dark pink, orange, white, yellow, turquoise, on white
Method
1. Book in hand extends above backdrop
2. Skirts are full sheets of tissue paper gathered together at waist with needle and thread
3. Ribbon ties to hide gathers
4. Hair is one hank of twisted wool yarn
5. Paper pasted on segment of doily, for necklace
6. Gold tassel pinned on where ribbon ties

Fred Worthington Photo

FIRST AID FOR THE AILING HOU[S]
Branch, The Enoch Pratt Free Library

(Final E not caught by camera)

Materials and Colors

    Cardboard, fabric, paint, [con]struction paper, ink

    Red, olive green, magenta, bl[ack] white, blue, yellow

Method

1. House cut from red cardbo[ard]
2. Brick lines painted on [white] edge of cardboard dipped [in] white paint
3. Plain, patterned, and strip[ed] fabrics used for overalls, s[...] and curtains, respectively
4. Paint on buckets, globs [of] real white poster paint
5. Lettering forming "roof" an [in]tegral part of poster's desig[n]

Sussman-Ochs Ph[oto]

PAMPHLET PARADE
The Enoch Pratt Free Library

Materials and Colors

    Assorted pamphlets, cardboard, cutout letters

    Brown, turquoise, tan and white

Method

1. "Feet" representing readers of various ages cut from cardboard
2. The narrow cardboard strips help unify the material, adding to the "parade" impression

Sussman-Ochs Photo

BOOKS ON BOATING

Materials and Colors
    Square-shaped sponge, paint, round
    sponge, paper, cardboard
    White, reds, black, on gray
Method
    1. "Water" done with square-shaped
        sponge and white paint
    2. Clouds done with round sponge and
        paint
    3. Large paper book makes one of the
        sails
    4. Fish, flags, sails, boat cut from paper
    5. Pole done with black paint, printed with
        edge of cardboard strip (a piece of
        rope may be substituted)

Fred Worthington Photo

BOOKS AND IDEAS IN AN AGE OF ANXIETY
Title taken from Institute, The Enoch Pratt Free Library

Materials and Colors
    Cardboard, construction paper, ink
    Black, light and dark pinks, on white
Method
    1. Ink lines for pages, pen pulled across
        paper with a jerky movement

Fred Worthington Photo

WINTER SPORTS

Materials and Colors

Construction paper, tissue paper, rubber cement, ink

White, pale tan, black, purple, light blue

Method

1. Figure cut from paper and pasted down
2. Book and birds drawn on, lettering done in black ink
3. Tissue attached, after cutting out area for book
4. Water area, particularly, must be wet well with thin cement, and tissue applied quickly, so lettering will show through

Fred Worthington Photo

HAVE BOOK, WILL TRAVEL

Materials and Colors

Construction paper, cardboard, crayon, poster paint, ink

Black, pink, orange, blue-lavender, on white

Method

1. Poster paints used for illustration
2. Cardboard edges dipped in paint for dark lines
3. Crayon used for lines indicating book pages
4. Real travel tags and stickers may be used instead of simulated items

Fred Worthington Photo

BIRD BEHAVIOR

Materials and Colors

Feathers, glitter, sequins, beads, cardboard, construction paper, tissue, glue, paint, tag board, typing paper

Pink, turquoise, pale green, purple, reds, on black cardboard

Method

1. Birds cut from white construction and tissue paper, and later attached
2. Feathers applied to wings, birds glued down, cage lines formed by dipping edge of cardboard strip in white poster paint
3. Miniature books made from tag board scored in the middle, white typing paper cut to same size, three or four pieces glued together in center, leaving pages free
4. Hole cut in cardboard and beads tied in knot at top

Fred Worthington Photo

FANTASY

Materials and Colors

Cardboard, transparent inks, crayon, tissue, pen and ink

Green, blue, pink, orange, on white

Fred Worthington Photo

BOOKS FOR A RAINY DAY

Materials and Colors

Cardboard, construction paper, crayon, ink
Magenta, olive green, yellow-orange,
black, on white

Method

1. Umbrella, arms, cut from paper
2. Fingers holding umbrella handle are left
   free
3. Books cut from cardboard and pinned
   away from background, to give raised
   effect
4. Lines for rain drawn with sharp-pointed
   crayon
5. Broken lines done with ruler and felt-
   tip pen

Fred Worthington Photo

HISTORICAL NOVELS

Materials and Colors

Felt roller, paint, cardboard, chalk, paper
Pale olive, vivid orange, magenta, white,
black

Method

1. Pale olive and thick white paint are
   rolled on blackboard, to give texture
   resembling old wall
2. Statue drawn on with chalk, then covered with white paint
3. Paper "leaves" pasted on head over
   paint
4. Paper book also pasted on

Fred Worthington Photo

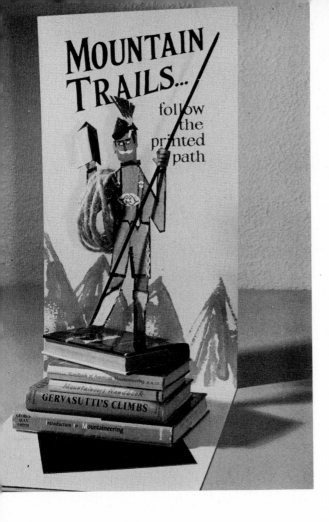

MOUNTAIN TRAILS

Materials and Colors

Paint, cardboard, real books (or book jackets stuffed with book discards), dowel stick, construction paper, rope

Blues, greens, pale purple for background mountains, black, white

Method

1. Bavarian mountain climber, cut from cardboard and decorated with brush and paint
2. Cardboard cut to size, lettered, and mountains painted on; then scored and bent, so that the lower portion serves as a platform for the pile of books. Easel attached to back enables it to stand free
3. Real rope on climber's arm, dowel stick glued into bent paper hand; 3-D bent paper and cardboard book glued into other hand
4. One foot pulled forward on top book, one foot on lower book, to give feeling of climbing and height

Note: This is a good poster to use in small areas, or where wall display space is lacking

Sussman-Ochs Photo

MIDDLE EAST
The Enoch Pratt Free Library

Materials and Colors

Paint roller, cardboard, wooden shelf, cutout letters, books

White, yellow, orange, purple, pink

Method

1. Paint rolled on rough surface gives sandy look (this wallboard backdrop was painted over so many times the surface was cracked, so instead of discarding, it was used for interesting texture)
2. Flat painted background, repeating two of the architectural shapes in cardboard, to give 3-D effect

Book shelf attached to backdrop, holding related books

Fred Worthington Photo

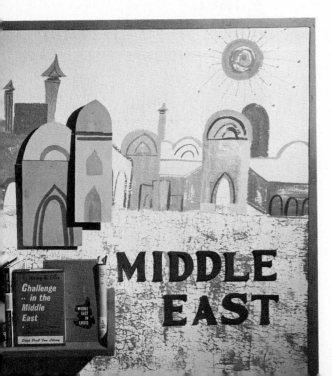

YOUNG ADULTS
Branch Section Heading, The Enoch Pratt Free Library

Materials and Colors
    Cardboard, cloth adhesive tape, ink
    Light oranges, yellow ochres, dull in tone
    Olive green letters

Method
1. Wide letter panels cut, remaining panels one-half their width
2. Panels taped together, so signs can stand free, accordion-fashion
3. Letter panels light; separation panels in darker tones

Sussman-Ochs Photo

DECORATIVE PAMPHLET BOXES
Branch, The Enoch Pratt Free Library

Plain black when purchased, hand-lettered signs are attached to the front, and brightly-colored cardboard sides added.

Panel at left, black lettering on buff; center panel, white on green; right panel, black lettering on orange cardboard, with white lines

Sussman-Ochs Photo

MORE FUN IN THE SUN
Enoch Pratt Free Library

Materials and Colors
 Cardboard figurines, cardboard rectangle and strips, cutout letters, mounted on wallboard
 Aqua, tangerine, white, imperial blue

Method
1. The two central baseball figures were cut from a whisky display piece obtained from a Baltimore tavern—an example of free commercial display materials which may be converted to library purposes
2. Other sports figures cut from cardboard with Cutawl machine

Fred Worthington Photo

GROW A BETTER GARDEN

Materials and Colors
 Cardboard, book jackets, cutout letters, paint
 Black, bright green, pink, white

Method
1. Flower petals, stems and leaves cut from cardboard, in identical patterns, but different colors. Leaves at right have white line inserts, omitted from design at left
2. Cardboard circles superimposed on petals hold them together, and form flower centers

Sussman-Ochs Photo

FREE-STANDING FLOWERS

Materials and Colors

Variegated construction paper, cardboard circle[s]
cardboard leaves, sticks and blocks of wood painte[d]
olive green (same color as leaves)
Black, magenta, red, orange, olive green, pin[k]
yellow orange, blue, green, purple, turquoise

Method

1. Sticks cut to desired heights and glued into hole[s]
   made in wooden bases
2. Slots for flowers cut into tops of sticks with [a]
   file
3. Black circles decorated with paper petals an[d]
   centers, pinned on
4. Each "flower" is then inserted in top slot [of]
   "stem," and cardboard leaves are thumb-tacke[d]
   on to backs of stick-stems

Sussman-Ochs Pho[to]

AMERICAN ART WEEK

Materials and Colors

Wood-grain cardboard, white
cardboard, paints
Browns, grays, various bright
colors, on white

Method

1. Cardboard wood-grain frame
2. Painted easel
3. Picture shown was done with water colors, bu[t a]
   print of a well-known painting, or picture cut fro[m a]
   discarded magazine, could also be used
4. Cutout letters may be pinned on after print i[s]
   glued down

164

Fred Worthington Pho[to]

APPENDIX

FOR SELECTIVE DISPLAY TIE-INS,
CONSULT THE FOLLOWING CALENDARS:

Chases' Calendar of Annual Events
Apple Tree Press, Publishers
2322 Mallery Street,
Flint 4, Mich.

The Children's Book Council, Inc.
Quarterly Calendar
175 Fifth Avenue,
New York 10, N. Y.

"Anniversaries and Holidays,"

by Mary E. Hazeltine

(If this book is available in the library)

SOURCES OF SUPPLY and EQUIPMENT

NOTE: This information may prove helpful to workers who do not have access to local display supply houses. The list is in no way complete, representing only firms with which the author has dealt directly, or learned about indirectly. A majority of those listed will furnish catalogs and prices on request.

ACETATE (.005)

Becker Sign Supply Company
321 N. Paca Street
Baltimore 1, Md.

Hubbs & Corning Company
404 S. Eutaw Street
Baltimore 1, Md.

Nyborgs'
117 W. Franklin Street
Baltimore 1, Md.

ANGEL HAIR

Permalife Glass Fiber Division
Box 6356
San Antonio 9, Tex.

ARTIFICIAL FLOWERS, GRASS, ETC.

Allied Display Materials, Inc.
241 W. 23rd Street
New York, N. Y.

Becker Sign Supply Company
321 N. Paca Street
Baltimore 1, Md.

The L. J. Charrot Company, Inc.
36 W. 37th Street
New York, N. Y.

Chingos & Sons, Inc.
818-20 Avenue of Americas
New York 1, N. Y.

Colonial Decorative Display
Company, Inc.
122 W. 26th Street
New York, N. Y.

Eaton Brothers Corporation
Display Division
Hamburg, N. Y.

Some dime, department stores

ARTISTS' SUPPLIES

Grand Central Artists' Materials, Inc.
3 East 40th Street
New York 16, N. Y.

The Hirshberg Company
214 W. Franklin Street
Baltimore 1, Md.

The Ohio Art Materials Company
2174 E. 9th Street
Cleveland 15, O.

Rogers Artists' Supply Company
225 W. Mulberry Street
Baltimore 1, Md.

BOOK WEEK POSTERS, STREAMERS

The Children's Book Council, Inc.
175 Fifth Avenue
New York 10, N. Y.

BRUSHES (Paint, Sign)

Becker Sign Supply Company
321 N. Paca Street
Baltimore 1, Md.

The Hirshberg Company
214 W. Franklin Street
Baltimore 1, Md.

The Ohio Art Materials Company
2174 E. 9th Street
Cleveland 15, O.

Rogers Artists' Supply Company
225 W. Mulberry Street
Baltimore 1, Md.

Underwood Supply Company
820 S. Hoover Street
Los Angeles 5, Calif.

BULLETIN BOARDS

Demco Library Supplies
Madison 1, Wis.
Fresno, Calif.
New Haven 2, Conn.

Fordham Equipment Company
2377-79 Hoffman Street
New York 58, N. Y.

Gaylord Library Supplies
155 Gifford Street
Syracuse, N. Y.
29 N. Aurora Street
Stockton, Calif.

Library Bureau
Remington Rand
315 Fourth Avenue
New York 10, N. Y.

CARDBOARD, 3 to 14 ply, 22"x 28"; 28"x44"; (Some display supply houses carry sheets 40"x 60", 14 ply and heavier, in white and colors)

Barton Duer & Koch Paper Company
81 W. Mosher Street
Baltimore 17, Md.

Becker Sign Supply Company
321 N. Paca Street
Baltimore 1, Md.

Crescent Cardboard Company
1240 North Homan
Chicago 51, Ill.

Hurlock Brothers Company, Inc.
3436 Market Street
Philadelphia 4, Pa.

The Mudge Paper Company
1400 Russell Street
Baltimore 30, Md.

National Card Mat & Board Company
4318 Carroll Avenue
Chicago 24, Ill.
11422 S. Broadway
Los Angeles 61, Calif.

Radiant Color Company
830 Isabella Street
Oakland 7, Calif.

CHALK (White and colored)

The Hirshberg Company
214 W. Franklin Street
Baltimore 1, Md.

Rogers Artists' Supply Company
225 W. Mulberry Street
Baltimore 1, Md.

CONSTRUCTION PAPER
(See also PAPER)

Paul M. Adams Company
4111 Washington Boulevard
Baltimore 3, Md.

Barton Duer & Koch Paper Company
81 W. Mosher Street
Baltimore 17, Md.

The Mudge Paper Company
1400 Russell Street
Baltimore 30, Md.

CRAYONS

Bogue Pencil Company
Yonkers, N. Y.

The Hirshberg Company
214 W. Franklin Street
Baltimore 1, Md.

The Sargent-Gerke Company
Indianapolis 6, Ind.

CUTAWL MACHINE

Becker Sign Supply Company
321 N. Paca Street
Baltimore 1, Md.

The Cutawl Corporation
Bethel, Conn.

DECORATIVE MATERIALS
(Foils, etc.)

Becker Sign Supply Company
321 N. Paca Street
Baltimore 1, Md.

The National Research Bureau, Inc. (Pin-up Santa Claus, 4' high)
415 N. Dearborn Street
Chicago 10, Ill.

DECORATIVE MATERIALS
(Foils, etc.)—(Continued)

R. A. Ohlhorst
278 Johnston Avenue
Jersey City 4, N. J.

Research Products Corporation
1015 E. Washington Avenue
Madison 1, Wis.

Sherman Paper Products (Pictorials, backgrounds, accessories)
Newton Upper Falls 64, Mass.
220 E. 42nd Street
Room 2513
New York, N. Y.
1414 S. Wabash Avenue
Chicago, Ill.

DISPLAY EQUIPMENT
(Peg board, portable units)

Demco Library Supplies
Madison 1, Wis.
Fresno, Calif.
New Haven 2, Conn.

Fearon Publishers, Inc.
2263 Union Street
San Francisco 23, Calif.

Gaylord Library Supplies
155 Gifford Street
Syracuse, N. Y.
29 N. Aurora Street
Stockton, Calif.

Ivel Construction Corporation
53rd Street and First Avenue
Brooklyn 32, N. Y.

(Business Service Bureau)
Masonite Corporation
Suite 2037
111 W. Washington Street
Chicago 2, Ill.

Charles Mayer Studios, Inc.
Bowery at Center
Akron 8, O.
Polecats, Inc.
Old Saybrook, Conn.

FABRICS

Frankel Associates, Inc. (Display fabrics and novelties)
56 West 45th Street
New York, N. Y.

Maharam Fabric Corporation
(Display fabrics and accessories)
130 West 46th Street
New York, N. Y.
412-20 N. Orleans Street
Chicago, Ill.
1113 S. Los Angeles
Los Angeles, Calif.

Utrecht Linens (Monk's cloth and similar weaves)
119 W. 57th Street
New York 19, N. Y.

Van Arden Fabrics, Inc. (Burlaps in plains and prints)
9 N. Moore Street
New York 13, N. Y.

Also, department and dime stores

FEATHERS

South African Feather Company, Inc.
1015 Filbert Street
Philadelphia 7, Pa.

FELT-TIP PENS

The Hirshberg Company
214 W. Franklin Street
Baltimore 1, Md.

Rogers Artists' Supply Company
225 W. Mulberry Street
Baltimore 1, Md.

Julius M. Stark & Company
202-206 Water Street
Baltimore 2, Md.

FIXATIVES
(Spray-type transparent protective coating)

Demo Library Supplies
Madison 1, Wis.
Fresno, Calif.
New Haven 2, Conn.

(Krylon)

Becker Sign Supplies
321 N. Paca Street
Baltimore 1, Md.

(Krylon)—(Continued)

Nyborgs'
117 W. Franklin Street
Baltimore 1, Md.

(Shellac)

Rogers Artists' Supply Company
225 W. Mulberry Street
Baltimore 1, Md.

Priceless Paint and Hardware
Company
214 W. Saratoga Street
Baltimore 1, Md.

FLAGS

Flág Banner & Pennant Shop
409 Park Avenue
Baltimore 1, Md.

FOREIGN ARTICLES (Wicker baskets, coasters, decorative items from abroad)

People's Super Market Imports
Company
2906 Garrison Boulevard
Baltimore 16, Md.

GLUE

The Borden Company (Elmer's
Glue-All)
New York, N. Y.

Delkote, Inc. (Delkote)
Wilmington, Del.
Berkeley, Calif.

Morningstar-Paisley, Inc. (#65-4180)
630 W. 51st Street
New York 19, N. Y.
1770 Canalport Avenue
Chicago 16, Ill.

HISTORIC MATERIALS

News Items — Front pages of
American history: The Battle of
Fort Sumter; Lee's Surrender; Lincoln's Assassination; The Chicago
Fire; The Explosion of the Maine;
Dewey's Victory at Manila Bay;
McKinley Shot; The San Francisco
Earthquake; Declaration of War
against Germany; Peace, World
War I

National Textbook Corporation
814 N. Michigan Avenue
Chicago 11, Ill.

Plaques — Declaration of Independence, The Constitution of
the United States, The Gettysburg Address.

Historic Plaques
P. O. Box 735
Evanston, Ill.

IMITATION FOODS

The Imitation Food Display
197 Waverly Avenue
Brooklyn 5, N. Y.

National Display Materials
65 N. 6th Street
Brooklyn 11, N. Y.

INKS

Becker Sign Supply Company
321 N. Paca Street
Baltimore 1, Md.

The Hirshberg Company
214 W. Franklin Street
Baltimore 1, Md.

Rogers Artists' Supply Company
225 W. Mulberry Street
Baltimore 1, Md.

The Sargent-Gerke Company
Indianapolis 6, Ind.

INSECT MODELS

Insect Model Company
410 Ogden Avenue
Fairmont, W. Va.

INSULITE (Smoothlite Wall Board)

Stebbins, Anderson
305 York Road
Baltimore 4, Maryland
Also, various lumber companies

JOB CHARTS

B'nai B'rith Vocational Service
1640 Rhode Island Avenue, N.W.
Washington 6, D. C.

LETTER CABINETS

Demco Library Supplies
Madison 1, Wis.
Fresno, Calif.
New Haven 2, Conn.

Fordham Equipment Company
2377-79 Hoffman Street
New York 58, N. Y.

Gaylord Library Supplies
155 Gifford Street
Syracuse, N. Y.
29 N. Aurora Street
Stockton, Calif.

LETTERS, LETTERING, LETTER PATTERNS

A. B. C. Pattern & Stencil Company ("For all layout purposes")
207 Willard Avenue
Michigan City, Ind.

Artype, Inc. Barrington, Ill.
(Transparent, self-adhering, acetate sheets of alphabets, numerals, symbols, etc.)

Austen Display (Gold letters)
133 W. 19th Street
New York 11, N. Y.

Becker Sign Supply Company (A variety of letter styles)
321 N. Paca Street
Baltimore 1, Md.

Arthur Brown & Bro., Inc. ("Transfers from carrying sheet with light pressure")
2 W. 46th Street
New York 36, N. Y.

Columbia Sign Equipment Company (Diversity of patterns)
Columbia, Pa.

Demco Library Supplies (Magnetic Dayglo, for metal peg board panel; gummed letter sign kit;

Profile letters, self-adhering plastic; Stik-On strips, plastic to protect label inserts)
Box 1488
Madison 1, Wis.
Box 1772
New Haven 2, Conn.
Box 852
Fresno, Calif.

Display Craft (Wood and plastic letters)
804 W. Main Street
Portland, Ind.

Faulkner Laboratories (Plastic letters, "sizes ¼" to 8")
4504 E. Hillsborough Avenue
Tampa 10, Fla.

Fort Hill Plastic Letters Corporation (Plexiglas letters)
Dept. S 82
40 Hanover Street
Boston 13, Mass.

Gaylord Library Supplies
155 Gifford Street
Syracuse, N. Y.
29 N. Aurora Street
Stockton, Calif.

Grace Letter Company (Graforel letters from France, "18 different styles")
77 Fifth Avenue
New York 3, N. Y.

Grand Central Artists' Materials, Inc. (Hernard "3-Dimensional display letters")
3 E. 40th Street
New York 16, N. Y.

Hallcraft Die-Cut Letters
2930 N. Eleventh Street
Philadelphia 33, Pa.

The Holes-Webway Company (Stick letters on gummed mounting strips)
St. Cloud, Minn.

Lynn—Sign Moulded Plastic Company (Moulded plastic letters, figures)
230 Albany Street
Cambridge 39, Mass.

LETTERS, LETTERING, LETTER PATTERNS—(Continued)

Mitten's Display Letters
2 West 46th Street
New York 36, N. Y.

Mutual Aids
1946 Hillhurst Avenue
Los Angeles 27, Calif.

Redicut Letter Company
6519 West Boulevard
Inglewood, Calif.

Red Wing Products (Large letters, printed red on white)
New Hyde Park, N. Y.

Watkins Metalcrafts, Inc. (Metal letters)
2251 E. 75th Street
Chicago 49, Ill.

MAT KNIFE

Becker Sign Supply Company
321 N. Paca Street
Baltimore 1, Md.

The Hirshberg Company
214 W. Franklin Street
Baltimore 1, Md.

Rogers Artists' Supply Company
225 W. Mulberry Street
Baltimore 1, Md.

MODELING, MOLDING MATERIALS

American Cynamid Company (Celastic)
609 Schuyler Avenue
Kearny, N. Y.

Grand Central Artists' Materials, Inc. (Plastelene)
3 E. 40th Street
New York 16, N. Y.

The Sargent-Gerke Company (Clay)
Indianapolis 6, Ind.

Also, some display supply houses

MOUNTING MATERIALS

Cel-U-Dex Corporation (Self-adhesive label holder)
New Windsor
Newburgh, N. Y.

Color Craft Corporation (Polyvinyl acetate)
819 S. Caroline Street
Baltimore 31, Md.

Gilbert Plastics and Supply Company (Polyvinyl acetate, colored plastics)
4300 E. Monument Street
Baltimore 5, Md.

Seal, Inc. (Seal dry mounting process)
Shelton, Conn.

NATIONAL LIBRARY WEEK AIDS

National Library Week (Posters, pennants, counter-cards, bookmarks, mobiles, "table tents")
P. O. Box 700
Great Neck
Long Island, N. Y.

NEWBERY - CALDECOTT MEDAL ENLARGEMENTS

The Children's Book Council, Inc.
175 Fifth Avenue
New York 10, N. Y.

PAINT ROLLERS

Priceless Paint & Hardware Company
214 W. Saratoga Street
Baltimore 1, Md.
Most hardware stores.

PAINTS

The American Crayon Company (Prang Tempera showcard colors)
Sandusky, O.
New York, N. Y.

Becker Sign Supply Company (Bulletin, Iddings, and others)
321 N. Paca Street
Baltimore 1, Maryland

PAINTS—(Continued)

Bienfang Products Corporation
(Artone Tempera colors)
Metuchen, N. J.

Consumers Paint Factory, Inc.
(Art and sign poster colors)
Gary, Ind.

The Hirshberg Company
214 W. Franklin Street
Baltimore 1, Md.

Iddings Paint Co., Inc. (Crown
Tempera colors, water paint)
Long Island City 1, N. Y.
Los Angeles 23, Calif.

Priceless Paint & Hardware Company (Bulletin and others)
214 W. Saratoga Street
Baltimore 1, Md.

Radiant Color Company (Fluorescent)
830 Isabella Street
Oakland 7, Calif.

Rogers Artists' Supply Company
225 W. Mulberry Street
Baltimore 1, Md.

Louis Sappanos Company
1617-23 North Ogden Avenue
Chicago 14, Ill.

The Sargent-Gerke Company
Indianapolis 6, Ind.

PAPER

(Construction)
The Paul M. Adams Company
4111 Washington Boulevard
Baltimore 3, Md.

Barton Duer & Koch Paper Company
81 W. Mosher Street
Baltimore 17, Md.

The Mudge Paper Company
1400 Russell Street
Baltimore 30, Md.
(Corrugated)

Becker Sign Supply Company
321 N. Paca Street
Baltimore 1, Md.

(Patterned—knotty pine, marble, etc.)

Becker Sign Supply Company
321 N. Paca Street
Baltimore 1, Md.

("Cutocolor" — adheshive sheets)
Bourges Color Corporation
80 Fifth Avenue
New York 11, N. Y.

(Seamless — 107" wide, in many colors)

Bulkley Dunton & Company, Inc.
Corry, Pa.

Also, various display supply houses.
(Tissue Sheets — in rolls)

East House Enterprises, Inc.
1075 First Avenue
New York 22, N. Y.

The Hirshberg Company
214 W. Franklin Street
Baltimore 1, Md.

PAPER CUTTERS

Becker Sign Supply Company
321 N. Paca Street
Baltimore 1, Md.

Gaylord Library Supplies
155 Gifford Street
Syracuse, N. Y.
29 N. Aurora Street
Stockton, Calif.

The Hirshberg Company
214 West Franklin Street
Baltimore 1, Md.

PENCILS (Color)

The Hirshberg Company
214 West Franklin Street
Baltimore 1, Md.

Julius Stark & Company
202-206 Water Street
Baltimore 2, Md.

PENNANTS

Central Flag & Banner Company
P.O. Box 1044
Rossmoyne, O.

PENNANTS—(Continued)

Flag Banner & Pennant Shop
409 Park Avenue
Baltimore 1, Md.

PENS

Becker Sign Supplies
321 N. Paca Street
Baltimore 1, Md.

C. Howard Hunt Pen Company
Camden 1, N. J.

PERMAFILM (Transparent, self-adhering protective coating)

The Columbia Sign Maker Company
Columbia, Pa.

PINS (Varied sizes)

Becker Sign Supply Company
321 N. Paca Street
Baltimore 1, Md.

Lucas Brothers, Inc.
221 W. Baltimore Street
Baltimore 2, Md.

PLIERS (Long-nosed)

Priceless Paint & Hardware Company
214 W. Saratoga Street
Baltimore 1, Md.
Most hardware stores.

PRINTS, POSTERS

American Angus Association (Angus cattle pictures, in color, free)
3201 Frederick Boulevard
St. Joseph, Mo.

Haddon Wood Ivins (Libri-Posters)
214 W. Second Street
Plainfield, N. J.

Regent Book Company (Children's posters and color prints)
1321 Viele Avenue
New York 59, N. Y.

PROJECTORS (Enlarging)

Rigyt-Damar
1341 S. Boston
Tulsa, Okla.

RUBBER CEMENT

The Hirshberg Company
214 W. Franklin Street
Baltimore 1, Md.

Rogers Artists' Supply Company
205 W. Mulberry Street
Baltimore 1, Md.

Union Rubber and Asbestos Company
Trenton, N. J.

RUBBER CEMENT DISPENSER

The Hirshberg Company
214 W. Franklin Street
Baltimore 1, Md.

Rogers Artists' Supply Company
225 W. Mulberry Street
Baltimore 1, Md.

RUBBER CEMENT THINNER

The Hirshberg Company
214 W. Franklin Street
Baltimore 1, Md.

Rogers Artists' Supply Company
225 W. Mulberry Street
Baltimore 1, Md.

SHELLAC (Clear)

Priceless Paint and Hardware Company
214 W. Saratoga Street
Baltimore 1, Md.

Rogers Artists' Supply Company
225 W. Mulberry Street
Baltimore 1, Md.

SIGN SUPPLIES

Becker Sign Supply Company
321 N. Paca Street
Baltimore 1, Md.

Dick Blick Company
Galesburg, Ill.

SIGN SUPPLIES—(Continued

Cappy & Company, Inc.
323 Boulevard of Allies
Pittsburgh 22, Pa.

Bert L. Daily, Inc.
126 E. 3rd Street
Dayton, O.

Martin Supply Company, Inc.
619 W. Franklin Street
Baltimore 1, Md.

SKETCHO (Crayon-like stick giving appearance of oil paint)

Grand Central Artists' Materials, Inc.
3 E. 40th Street
New York 16, N. Y.

Also, many other art supply houses

"SNOW"

Claremont Flock Corporation
1440 N. Halsted Street
Chicago, Ill.

Frostee Sno Company
Antioch, Ill.

U. S. Mica Company, Inc.
26 Sixth Street
Stamford, Conn.

Also, Instant Ivory Soap Flakes, from grocery stores and supermarkets.

SOAP ERASERS (Art gum)

Becker Sign Supplies
321 N. Paca Street
Baltimore 1, Md.

The Hirshberg Company
214 W. Franklin Street
Baltimore 1, Md.

Rogers Artists' Supply Company
225 W. Mulberry Street
Baltimore 1, Md.

SPONGES

The Hirshberg Company
214 West Franklin Street
Baltimore 1, Md.

Rogers Artists' Supply Company
225 W. Mulberry Street
Baltimore 1, Md.

Also, utility, dime stores.

STYROFOAM

Arts and Crafts Supply Company
(Styrofoam sheets)
321 Park Avenue
Baltimore 1, Md.

Some florist shops and dime stores (Styrofoam balls)

TACKERS (Staplers)

Arrow Fastener Company, Inc.
1 Junius Street
Brooklyn 12, N. Y.

Becker Sign Supply Company
321 N. Paca Street
Baltimore 1, Md.

A. L. Hansen Manufacturing Company
5041 Ravenswood Avenue
Chicago 40, Ill.

TAPE

Becker Sign Supply Company
(Clear, color, masking)
321 N. Paca Street
Baltimore 1, Md.

Chesapeake Tape Company
(Double-coated cloth adhesive)
Box 3535
Baltimore 14, Md.

Demco Library Supplies (Fastape, self-adhesive cloth)
Madison 1, Wis.
Fresno, Calif.
New Haven 2, Conn.

Fordham Equipment Company
2377-79 Hoffman Street
New York 58, N. Y.

The Hirshberg Company (Clear, color, masking)
214 W. Franklin Street
Baltimore 1, Md.

Nyborgs' (Clear, color)
117 W. Franklin Street
Baltimore 1, Md.

TAPE—(Continued)

Priceless Paint and Hardware Company ("Mystic" adhesive cloth, various widths and colors)
214 W. Saratoga Street
Baltimore 1, Md.

Rogers Artists' Supply Company (Clear, color, masking)
225 W. Mulberry Street
Baltimore 1, Md.

Wick Narrow Fabric Company (White cotton, on 1,000 yard spools)
112 N. Twelfth Street
Philadelphia, Pa.

THUMB TACKS

Hardware, dime, stationery, art supply stores.

UNITED NATIONS EXHIBIT KIT
(Also suitable for displays relating to the United States and foreign affairs, human rights, world problems, Brotherhood Week, etc.)

Oceana Publications, Inc.
40 Cedar Street
Dobbs Ferry, N. Y.

UPHOLSTERY TACKS

Hardware, furniture - related, some dime stores.

VACATION READING KIT

The Children's Book Council
175 Fifth Avenue
New York 10, N. Y.

SOME RELATED READINGS

BOOKS

Benson, John Howard, and
Carey, Arthur Graham
The Elements of Lettering, 2d ed.

Biegeleisen, Jacob Israel
ABC of Lettering

Buckley, Robert D.
A Basic Guide to Lettering

Cataldo, John W.
Lettering: A Guide for Teachers

Coplan, Kate
Effective Library Exhibits: How to Prepare and Promote Good Displays

Duvall, Edward J.
The Show Card Writer

East, Marjorie
Display for Learning, edited by Edgar Dale

Games, Abram
Over My Shoulder

George, Ross Frederick
Speedball Text Book; Lettering, Poster Design for Pen or Brush, 17th ed.

Holme, Rathbone
Modern Lettering and Calligraphy

Holmes, Carl
ABC of Lettering

Holub, Rand
Lettering Simplified

Horn, George
Bulletin Boards

Johnson, Pauline
Creating with Paper

Leach, Mortimer
Lettering for Advertising

Matthews, E. C.
Sign Painting Course

Meijer, M.
Script Lettering

Randall, Reino
Bulletin Boards and Display

Ruby, Doris
4D Bulletin Boards That Teach

Schoenoff, Herbert A.
Poster Making in the Elementary School

Stevens, Donald
Brush Script

Waugh, Dorothy
Festive Decoration the Year Round

BOOKLETS, ARTICLES

Baumgarner, A.A.D.
Questions You Ask
Sch Arts 59:55 F '60

Biegeleisen, Jacob Israel
Professional Lettering; excerpt from ABC of Lettering
Design 60:70-2 N '58

Blanchard, Julia G.
Something Old, Something New . . . with list of sources of free and inexpensive display materials
Wilson Lib Bul 35:634-40 Ap '61

Bradbury, Alice Libby
College Peps Up Poster Designing
Sch Arts 56:33 F '57

Buehner, Alice
Trace Day
Baltimore Bulletin of Education, Vol. XXXVIII No. 3:19-22

Calder, Dorothy
We'll Do It If We Can Use Our Heads; art class of Decatur, Ga. High School
Sch Arts 57:33-4 O '57

Campanella, James T.
Let's Dress Up Our Bulletin Boards
Ind Arts & Voc Educ 43:291-2 O '54

Can You Use A Bulletin Board?
Sunset 110:120-1 Ap '53

Cooke, Emma Ellen
Versatile Bulletin Board
Nat Educ Assn J 41:579 D '52

Defourny, John J.
Are You Using Your Bulletin Board?
Ind Arts & Voc Educ 40:311 O '51

E-Z Bulletin Boards
Fearon Publishers

BOOKLETS, ARTICLES—(Continued)

East, Marjorie
Better Bulletin Boards
Prac Home Econ 4:40 F '59

East, Marjorie
Methods for Creating Persuasive Bulletin Boards
Prac Home Econ 4:13 Mr '59

East, Marjorie
What Students Learn When They Create Bulletin Boards
Prac Home Econ 4:26 Ap '59

Emerson, Myrtle C.
Bulletin Board "Fever"; Camp Polk, La.
Lib J 79:184-5 F '54

Friese, Eugene
"Charlotte's Web"
Lib J 87:273-274 J15, '62

Gerstman, Maria K.
Art of Lettering
Sch Arts 51:24-5 S '51

Harbage, Mary
Sharing Time: Suggestions for Teachers of the Elementary Grades
Sr Sch 74:13 T Ap '59

Jahnke, Jeanne
Bulletin Board Displays
Wilson Lib Bul 33:499-503 Mr '59

Johnson, Fridolf
Educated Hand
Am Artist 21:49-54 S '57

Krogstad, Roland J.
Lettering Visual Aid
Ind Arts & Voc Educ 43:293 O '54

Kulp, Aimee K.
It Pays to Advertise! Mercersburg Academy Library
Lib J 78:664-8 Ap 15 '53

Noble, Ann and Oetting, Jeanette
Put Your Bulletin Boards to Work!
Prac Home Econ 33:36-7

Ottman, Sidney R.
Bored with Your Bulletin Board?
Nat Educ Assn J 43:286-7 My '54

Our Bulletin Board
Nat Educ Assn J 48:40-1 Mr '59

Pickett, Ann
"World" on Pegboard
Lib J 78:1284 Ag '53

Sargent, Mary Frances
Display and Decoration Ideas for the Recreation Leader
Recreation 50:294-6 O '57

Sasser, Elizabeth
Posters in the Round
Sch Arts 52:230-1 Mr '53

Shulze, Margaret M.
Those Bulletin Boards!
Lib J 78:668 Ap 15 '53

Stepat, Dorothy
How We Use Our Bulletin Board
Prac Home Econ 33:16 Ja '55

Strange, Elizabeth
Poster Planning
Sch Arts 52:226-8 Mr '53

Thresher, Roberta
Please, Mr. Principal, No More Posters!
Sch Arts 59:23-4 S '59

Todd, Jesse
Bulletin Boards for the Walls
Sch Arts 51:44 D '51

Turner, William Wirt and Others
Lettering Technique
Design 55:126-7 Ja '54

Weisjohn, Rhyllis
Bulletin Board Display
Wilson Lib Bul 34:569-83 Ap '60

What Makes A Poster? (Six experts unburden their minds)
Design 54:116-17 F '53

Wider, Stella E.
Poster Pointers
Sch Arts 51:22-3 S '51

Williams, Lucille
A Bulletin Board Speaks
Staff Newsletter, Baltimore Public Schools
Vol. XIV P. 6 Ja 3 '61

Willis, Hazel
Cut-Paper Letters Make Fine Posters
Sch Arts 57:20 D '57

Woodward, Jean L.
School Library Bulletin Board
Wilson Lib Bul 27:540-4 Mr '53

ABBREVIATIONS

Am Artist
American Artist

Ind Arts & Voc Educ
Industrial Arts & Vocational Education

Lib J
Library Journal

Nat Educ Assn J
National Education Association Journal

Prac Home Econ
Practical Home Economics

Sch Arts
School Arts

Sr Sch
Senior Scholastic

Wilson Lib Bul
Wilson Library Bulletin

#22
5c